LAW
for the Haulier

LAW
for the Haulier

Largent Brown
LLB, MCIT

KOGAN
PAGE

First published in Great Britain, 1987, by
Kogan Page Ltd
120 Pentonville Road, London N1 9JN

Copyright © Largent Brown 1987

British Library Cataloguing in Publication Data
Brown, Largent
  Law for the haulier.
  1. Trucking—Law and legislation—
  Great Britain
  I. Title
  344.1'0024388   KD2636
  ISBN 1-85091-147-9

Printed and bound in Great Britain by
Biddles Ltd, Guildford, Surrey

Contents

Acknowledgements

The preparation of this book has been helped, once more, by the kind assistance of officers of the Freight Transport Association at their headquarters in Tunbridge Wells. Members of the Road Haulage Association have also given useful critical comments. Discussions with John Hooper and Tony Pomeroy of the Transport Tutorial Association have been most fruitful. Naturally, constructive criticism from hauliers, too numerous to mention in this short note, has helped me to keep discussion of the law relatively uncomplicated. I should also like to thank Janet Scharf for applying her keen mind to the difficult task of editing such a book.

Lecturing to students on the Chartered Institute of Transport qualifying examination course on 'Law of Business and Carriage' run by the Polytechnic of North London has helped me to concentrate on areas which both hauliers and students find important and in need of clarification. Stuart Cole, Course Director for CIT courses at PNL, has encouraged me to adopt a practical approach towards legal problems likely to be encountered by the haulier, and this is the spirit in which this book has been prepared.

I am grateful to Overdrive for permission to reproduce their trading conditions which are a model of clarity and brevity. Copious references to case law have been avoided deliberately on the grounds that readers of a short introductory guide will be more concerned with legal principles. To assist further study, however, a list of references concludes the book and I am grateful to the various publishers for permission to make use of extracts from these works.

Finally, it is once again my great pleasure to thank Margery Stewart for her excellent typing of the manuscript.

Introduction

The typical haulage business in the UK has tended to operate on a small scale. Indeed, the owner-driver of a large heavy goods vehicle specializing in the carriage of frozen foods across the Continent, for instance, has a real future in the 1980s, even though the highly competitive rates offered by the big operators make it difficult for the small, non-specialist haulier to make enough profit to replace his vehicle and carry on in business.

A 'small firm' in the road haulage industry can reasonably be thought of as having five vehicles or less; ownership and management are usually centred on one person or a small group; coincidence and overlap of functions between owners and managers is common. Such firms are often dominated by a single family; they often supply a personal service to customers in one particular region; and difficulty in obtaining finance is recognized as a common problem.

While there are still thousands of small haulage firms operating in the UK, these are gradually giving way, in a keen business environment, to larger companies which can benefit from economies of scale. More and more hauliers are feeling the need to offer a complete transport, warehousing and contract distribution service.

For those small firms operating without the benefit of an in-house lawyer, the cost of obtaining legal advice is alleviated by the excellent services of the RHA and the FTA. But, to get the best out of any legal adviser, the haulier needs to have a reasonable understanding of the rules and regulations which govern his operations.

It is the aim of this book to provide the haulier with an understanding of the principles of law which affect the business and the way in which the courts tend to interpret those laws today. Students preparing for their Chartered Institute of Transport examinations should also benefit from this introductory volume.

Chapter 1
The Firm's Legal Structure

There is no special legal code for hauliers in the UK, but an awareness and understanding of legal powers and obligations is crucial to all operators. Obscurity of language used in legal company or partnership documents must never be an excuse for complacency on the subject of internal organization. Those who take advantage of trade association courses to keep up to date, and those who make the most of professional legal advice, are well rewarded.

From a legal point of view, a firm is considered to exist if hauling goods is carried on as a regular profit making activity, using assets such as business premises and involving two or more people, with some management direction and control. The existence of a firm has certain implications from the point of view of taxation as well as the law.

Making the right choice of legal structure for your haulage business is crucial. The decision to operate as a sole trader, as a partnership or as a limited company is one which should be made on the advice of a lawyer and an accountant who have a clear picture of your management objectives. It is not a decision which should ever be taken in a hasty or uninformed way: a wrong decision could have very serious consequences.

'Sole trader', for our purposes, means an unincorporated haulage business in which one person is the owner whether or not he has any employees. As a sole trader, the only special rule with which you need to comply is to use your own name to designate the business. Having a separate bank account for all haulage transactions and making sure that accounts are properly kept are obvious ways of ensuring the minimum interference from the Inspector of Taxes.

Partnerships are found quite often in the road haulage industry, often between members of one family who wish to keep business formalities to a minimum. The legal definition of a partnership (Partnership Act 1890) is 'the relationship which subsists between persons carrying on a business in common with a view to profit . . . entered into for a single adventure or undertaking'. Whereas a company is primarily an association of shareholders, a partnership is essentially a group of co-owners.

Many small businesses decide to forgo the practical benefits of company status, finding that partnership law is more suited to the regulation of a small business. The main disadvantage of a partnership arises from the rule that every partner is liable jointly with the other partners for all debts and obligations of the firm incurred while a partner. As the partners are the firm, their personal wealth is available to meet any claims against the partnership. If one partner by his actions attracts a liability to the firm, the others may have to contribute some of their own capital in the firm to discharge that liability. If a partner has little or no personal money to meet a claim against the firm, the other partners have to make good the loss, at whatever personal cost.

Limited liability is the most obvious advantage of being a member of a company rather than entering business as a partner or as a sole trader, and the private limited company is the structure which most haulage operators decide suits them best.

A private limited company may hold property in the corporate name, and usually finds it easier to attract loan finance than the sole trader or partnership. Perpetual succession, advantageous treatment of dismissed directors and a greater flexibility in the creation of ownership interests are all clear benefits arising from incorporation.

However, there are disadvantages to be considered. Forming a company in the first place involves a certain amount of work and expense. A company is obliged to comply with certain disclosure requirements, particularly the filing of annual audited accounts, which incur expense and possible prejudice. And shareholders and directors with an informal way of working together may find the procedures required by the company's constitution cumbersome and unattractive.

A private limited company comes into existence upon incorporation; that is, upon the filing of a Memorandum of Association with supporting documentation, and the issue of a certificate of incorporation by the Registrar of Companies.

The company's legal rights and duties are largely governed by its own rulebook or constitution, which comprises the Memorandum of Association and the Articles of Association.

Memorandum of Association

The Memorandum of Association would look like this:
1. The name of the company is Haultech Limited (commonly abbreviated to HLT).
2. The registered office of the company is in England and Wales to wit at the offices of Messrs Runne, Hoppit & Co solicitors of Great Gables, Jumps Lane, Newbury.

The name of the company must end with the word 'Limited' so that its nature is clear to all who deal with it. The second clause shows that the company is domiciled in England and Wales and is thus liable to pay British tax and to operate under British law. The address of the company solicitor or accountant is often used. The Registrar of Companies must be notified of any change.

The next item in the Memorandum is likely to be the 'objects clause'. It might read like this:
3. The objects for which the company is established are:
   (a) For the business of road haulage contractor more particularly for the specialist carriage of goods of a hi-tech nature throughout the United Kingdom, the member states of the European Economic Community, Switzerland, Austria, Norway, Sweden and the Warsaw Pact countries.
   (b) To carry on any other trade or business whatever which can in the opinion of the Board of Directors be advantageously carried on in connection with or ancillary to any of the businesses of the company.
   (c) To purchase or by any other means acquire and take options over any property whatever, and any rights or privileges of any kind over or in respect of any property.

The objects clause is often long, with many sub-clauses. But its aim is to be specific about the company's objectives without unnecessarily restricting its ability to carry on business in a sensible manner. If difficulties arise over interpretation of the objects clause, legal advice should be sought.

The Memorandum goes on to state:

4. The liability of the members is limited.

This means that if the company goes into liquidation, for whatever reason, the company's creditors will only obtain from the shareholders the amount still owed on their shares. This liability applies to all shareholders including the directors.

The next clause might read:

5. The share capital of the company is £100 divided into 100 shares of £1 each.

This relates to the initial nominal authorized capital. The clause can be altered to take account of new share issues and so on, but any alterations must be notified to the Registrar of Companies.

The Memorandum requires at least two signatories:

6. We, the several persons whose names and addresses are subscribed, are desirous of being formed into a company, in pursuance of this Memorandum of Association, and we respectively agree to take the number of shares in the capital of the company set opposite our respective names.

When you buy a company 'off the shelf', this subscription to the Memorandum will already have been made, perhaps by company formation agents such as Jordans. Existing subscribers will stand down once the company has been registered in your name.

Articles of Association

These cover the internal organization of the company. They incorporate the rules laid down in the Companies (Tables A–F) Regulations 1985. The rules are modified by the company to suit its particular requirements. The Articles of Association of our fictional company, Haultech Limited, contain the following headings:

- Allotment of shares
- Shares
- General meetings and resolutions

- Appointment of directors
- Borrowing powers
- Alternate directors
- Powers of directors
- Indemnity
- Additional powers
- Transfer of shares
- Removal of directors
- Enhanced voting rights for directors.

The language used in most Articles of Association is extremely complicated, and it may often be necessary to obtain legal help in deciphering it. It is worthwhile mentioning here a few points regarding the roles of directors and partners which are frequently misunderstood.

General responsibilities of directors

The sole trader can run his business just as he chooses, within the confines of the law. As the director of a company, or as a partner, you must not only take into account the views of your co-directors or partners, but you must act fairly and reasonably in your dealings with them. You are required to act both honestly and in the best interests of the firm. The courts are full of cases which have originated in the failure of a director or partner to account properly to his firm.

In the haulage business, for example, it is quite easy to convince oneself that a return load not originally contracted for should be regarded as a perk for the enterprising driver obtaining such a load. One reason why return loads are so poorly paid is that the drivers frequently receive a cash payment which, it is understood, will never find its way on to the company's books.

A director has to account for any profit made by him as a result of his company directorship. It is possible, however, for the members of a company to agree in general meeting that such profit may accrue to the director himself and not to his company. Even if a director obtains a haulage contract which it is doubtful could have been obtained by his company, he must account for profits. Lawyers like to compare directors with trustees in that they have a fiduciary relationship to their company; that is, they are held in special trust, in the performance of their duties. When in doubt as to his duties a director can always discuss his views at a board meeting, a course of action which has much to commend it on a practical note.

An an agent of the company, a director can only make contracts in accordance with the scope of the objects clause in the company's Memorandum of Association. If a director makes a haulage contract which is outside the scope of his company's objects clause, he will become personally liable on the contract; his company cannot be made liable. If a third party (the company and the director being the first and second parties) can show he acted in good faith even though the contract in question appears outside the powers of the haulage company, he can enforce the contract and the company will be liable. Provided that he is not aware of any specific limitations on the power of the company to make the haulage contract, the third party can enforce the contract. The third party need not even look into the company's power to contract or the power of the directors to bind the company.

Apart from looking after the interests of a company's members, company directors should also safeguard the well-being of a company's employees. In a typical small haulage company the practical implications of this duty are not very difficult to work out. In a large organization this duty can be quite complicated and specialist legal advice will probably be sought by the haulage company when setting up welfare schemes for the benefit of drivers and other company employees. The amount of skill to be exercised by a company director in the performance of his duties obviously varies with the size and complexity of the haulage company in question. In a famous fraud case, the following guidelines were put forward:

1. A company director need not show in the performance of his duties a greater degree of skill than may be reasonably expected from a person of his knowledge and experience.
2. A director need not give continuous attention to the affairs of his company. After all, his duties are of an occasional nature performed at board meetings etc. He should, however, attend meetings when he can

possibly do so.

3. Duties which may be properly delegated to an official, eg to the company secretary, may assume to be honestly carried out by such official.

The above minimum standards relate to non-executive directors. A greater degree of skill and commitment will naturally be expected of executive directors, particularly of the managing director.

Breach of duty

If a director is found to be in breach of duty there are certain remedies available to the aggrieved company, members and co-directors. A director who is an employee of the company may be summarily dismissed: even managing directors of haulage companies can be fired! As already mentioned, a director must account to his company for any profit made by him as director. If a board of directors is intent on taking action beyond the scope of its power, an injunction may be granted against the board to prevent a breach which is threatened. A director in breach of duty may have to pay damages to someone who has suffered loss as a result of the breach. A director guilty of fraudulent trading, whether or not winding-up proceedings have taken or are taking place, is subject to a criminal penalty. The question of breach of duty is regarded very seriously by the courts and any article of the company purporting to exclude a director from liability for such breach, also for breach of trust, default or negligence, has no legal effect. A director cannot rely on an exclusion clause to cover his own wrongdoing.

Board meetings

The running of a modern haulage company is carried out by its directors at board meetings throughout the year. The power of management is usually delegated by the shareholders to the board of directors in words such as these:

The business of the company shall be managed by the directors, who may exercise all such powers of the company as are not required to be exercised by the company in general meeting.

Once the power of management is vested collectively in the directors, it can be exercised only by the board of directors, which is controlled by the chairman.

Removal of directors

The Companies Act requires directors to offer themselves for re-election, and allows members to vote out directors by a simple majority. This applies to all companies, public and private, and all directors, except for a director for life appointed on or before 18 July 1945. A director must vacate his office in these circumstances:

- when he reaches the age of 70
- when he is made insolvent
- when he does not obtain his share qualification
- when he is prohibited from being a director having committed fraud and certain other criminal offences
- when he becomes mentally disturbed
- upon resignation (in writing)
- when he remains absent, without permission, from board meetings for over six months.

It is commonplace for a director to vacate his office to avoid a conflict of interest in a contract made by his company. After such a contract has been completed, there is nothing to stop the director being re-appointed if the company wishes to make use of his services once more. In some situations, especially upon retirement, a director may properly receive compensation for loss of office. The rules are a little complicated and an accountant's professional advice should be sought to ensure a mutually satisfactory form of compensation for the retiring director.

Remuneration of directors

Remuneration of directors is an area which seems to cause a lot of problems. The relevant Article usually reads as follows:

> The remuneration of the Directors shall from time to time be determined by the company in general meeting. Such remuneration shall be deemed to accrue from day to day. The Directors may also be paid all travelling, hotel and other expenses properly incurred by them in attending and returning from meetings of the Directors or any committee of

the Directors or general meetings of the company or in connection with the business of the company.

Being a director does not, in itself, carry entitlement to payment. The best course for a director is to have a proper service contract setting out all his benefits and conditions of work as an employee of the company. If a serious disagreement arises between directors, a director without a proper contract of service may be in a very vulnerable position.

The role of the managing director

The roles of individual directors are usually set out in great detail in the Articles of Association. Unfortunately, in the excitement of forming a company, little attention may be paid to these provisions, and reference is often not made to them until a dispute actually arises.

The role of managing director in particular often presents problems. By Article 109 of Table A:

> The directors may entrust to and confer upon a managing director any of the powers exercisable by them upon such terms and conditions and with such restrictions as they may think fit, and either collaterally with or to the exclusion of their own powers and may from time to time revoke, withdraw, alter or vary all or any of such powers.

Given the manifest importance of the managing director this division of directorial powers should be known.

Partnership

A partnership, unlike a company, has no legal existence apart from the individual partners working together for profit. Even without a formal partnership agreement, you can be regarded as a partner, if, for instance, you share in the profits.

Most partners have their working relationship set out in Articles of Partnership. When no such agreement exists, reference has to be made to the provisions of the Partnership Act. Particularly important are the rules contained in Section 24 of that Act. Subject to any agreement made between the partners, these rules cover the relationship between the partners in a firm:

1. All the partners are entitled to share equally in the capital and profits of the business, and must contribute equally towards the losses whether of capital or otherwise sustained by the firm.
2. The firm must indemnify every partner in respect of payments made and personal liabilities incurred by him:
   (a) in the ordinary and proper conduct of the business of the firm; or
   (b) in or about anything necessarily done for the preservation of the business or property of the firm.
3. A partner, making, for the purpose of the partnership, any actual payment or advance beyond the amount of capital which he has agreed to subscribe, is entitled to interest at the rate of 5 per cent per annum from the date of the payment or advance.
4. A partner is not entitled, before the ascertainment of profits, to interest on the capital subscribed by him.
5. Every partner may take part in the management of the partnership business.
6. No partner shall be entitled to remuneration for acting in the partnership business.
7. No person may be introduced as a partner without the consent of all existing partners.
8. Any difference arising as to ordinary matters connected with the partnership business may be decided by a majority of the partners, but no change may be made in the nature of the partnership business without the consent of all existing partners.
9. The partnership books are to be kept at the place of business of the partnership (or the principal place, if there is more than one), and every partner may, when he thinks fit, have access to and inspect and copy any of them.

As a general rule, all partners take a part in management, and it is wise to formalize the division of responsibilities. With three partners in a haulage firm, a typical arrangement is for one to have the main responsibility for administration, another for operational control and the third for sales. One partner should have the clear responsibility of maintaining a satisfactory cash flow. Failure to define this responsibility is the first step on the path to insolvency. Responsible decision making usually means that the senior partner abides by the will of the majority. If the partners ever have to go to the courts or to arbitration over a controversial decision, it may well be time for the haulage firm to review its direction and, perhaps, see if another business should be established. Trying to reach a decision by using a third party, which is often without any special knowledge of the haulage business in question, is rarely an adequate substitute for decision making in-house.

Partnership law makes the assumption that each partner takes an equal share in the profits or losses of the firm. If partners want a different arrangement they should set this out in writing in the clearest terms, preferably with the help of their solicitor.

One of the most common problem areas is the distinction between partnership and private property. If, for example, one of the partners allows his estate car to be used for business purposes (say, light parcel deliveries) in consideration for all car running expenses being met by the firm, does this arrangement make the car partnership property? If the car was being bought by hire purchase with the haulage firm making the repayments, this would certainly suggest it was partnership property. To avoid arguments over such matters, which can easily lead to very serious trouble between partners, it is essential to itemize personal and partnership property. This should be done whether or not there is a written partnership agreement on all general matters (rarely the case).

The auditor

It is the auditor's job to scrutinize all the company accounts and report on them to the shareholders. He decides whether proper returns have been kept by the company and submits his report, attached to the balance sheet, to the company secretary for publication in general meeting.

The auditor is also obliged to check that the company's securities do in fact exist and are in safe custody. He must also ensure that the company's true financial position is reflected in its books so that a proper valuation of its shares can be made if necessary.

This is how Lord Denning described the duties of an auditor in Fornento (Sterling Area) Ltd v Selsdon Fountain Pen Co Ltd:

> An auditor is not to be confused to the mechanics of checking vouchers and making arithmetical computations. He is not to be written off as a professional 'adder-upper and subtractor'. His vital task is to take care to see that errors are not made, be they errors of computation, or errors of commission or downright untruths. To perform this task properly, he must come to it with an enquiring mind – not suspicious of dishonesty, I agree – but suspecting that someone may have made a mistake somewhere and that a check must be made to ensure that there has been none.

If an auditor fails to discharge his duties in a professional manner, he is liable to the company for any loss or damage arising from this failure.

The company secretary

Every company must have a company secretary. A sole director cannot hold this office as well. In a typical family haulage company with husband and wife as the two directors, the wife takes on the title of company secretary.

Apart from signing the annual return and certifying accounts sent with the return, the company secretary has to prepare returns and keep the company registers in good order, making sure, for example, that all share transactions are properly completed.

A most important function is to give proper notice of company meetings, to prepare agendas for them, and to take the minutes. The company secretary is usually entrusted with the job of completing all post-meeting documentation.

Lord Denning, this time in Panorama Developments (Guildford) Ltd v Fidelis Furnishing Fabrics Ltd, describes the duties of a company officer most concisely:

> A company secretary is a much more important person than he was in 1887. . . . He is an officer of the company with extensive duties and responsibilities. This appears not only

in the modern Companies Acts, but also by the role which he plays in the day-to-day business of companies. He is no longer a mere clerk. He regularly makes representations on behalf of the company and enters into contracts on its behalf which come within the day-to-day running of the company's business. So much so that he may be regarded as held out as having authority to do such things on behalf of the company. He is certainly entitled to sign contracts connected with the administrative side of a company's affairs, such as employing staff, and ordering cars, and so forth. All such matters now come within the ostensible authority of a company's secretary.

The company secretary of Fidelis Furnishing Fabrics Ltd (in the case cited above) ordered cars from the car hire firm Panorama Developments on company stationery signing himself 'Company Secretary'. The cars were to carry important customers of Fidelis, said the fraudulent company secretary, who actually used the cars himself despite signing hiring agreements on behalf of Fidelis. The decision of the court was that Fidelis were liable for the hire of the cars as the company secretary did have ostensible authority to make contracts for the hire of cars.

As an officer of the company, the secretary is, of course, liable for failing to comply with his duties as laid down under the Companies Acts.

General meetings

Every company is obliged to hold an annual general meeting every calendar year. The usual business at an AGM is the consideration of the accounts and reports, election of directors, appointment of auditors and fixing of their fee, and approval of company dividends.

An extraordinary general meeting can be demanded upon special notice of 21 days by a group of shareholders (usually holding over 10 per cent of the voting shares in the company) if the directors are not prepared to call such a meeting. The directors normally have the power to call an extraordinary general meeting to deal with matters which cannot wait until the next AGM.

The other type of shareholders' meeting is a 'class meeting' for members holding a particular class of share. Such a meeting is usually held simply to agree changes to the rights of the class in question.

The many technical aspects of holding meetings are not within the scope of this book but can be found in any basic introduction to company law.

Chapter 2
Contracts

A business bargain or contract rests on the basic proposition that each party to the contract is in agreement. A contract has been defined as 'an agreement giving rise to obligations which are enforced or recognized by law'. Contractual obligations are distinguished from other legal obligations because of this fundamental notion of agreement.

However, there are qualifications to the above legal proposition. First, commercial convenience dictates that the law is frequently more concerned with the objective appearance of agreement rather than the actual fact of agreement, as was stated in an 1871 judgment:

> If, whatever a man's real intention may be, he so conducts himself that a reasonable man would believe that he was assenting to the terms proposed by the other party, and that other party upon that belief enters into a contract with him, the man thus conducting himself would be equally bound as if he had intended to agree to the other party's terms.

A second qualification to the basic proposition is that the parties to a contract are usually required to observe recognized standards of behaviour. These standards arise from terms implied by law. For example, a lorry driver implicitly undertakes that he is reasonably skilled as a driver. The haulier, for example, implicitly undertakes in the employment contract that he will not ask his drivers, or indeed any of his employees, to do an unlawful act.

A third qualification is that modern contracts are no longer based on the nineteenth-century notion of freedom of contract. Today economically more powerful contracting parties can impose their wishes on weaker parties by using standard form contracts. The appearance of agreement under a standard form agreement masks the reality of the weaker party having little freedom in practice in deciding whether to agree to the standard terms or not. A classic case is where parties contract on terms settled by a trade association. The

RHA Conditions of Carriage 1982 are a case in point.
Let us now turn to these RHA Conditions in some detail.

RHA Conditions of Carriage 1982

The form starts by establishing that the haulier using the RHA conditions accepts goods for haulage only on the terms contained in those conditions. There follows a definitions section. The form uses the words 'carrier' and 'carriage' rather than 'haulier' and 'haulage'. The buyer of haulage services (the customer) is referred to as the 'trader', and the goods carried by the carrier for the trader is the 'consignment'. The contract of carriage (haulage) made between the carrier and the trader is simply called the 'contract'. 'Dangerous goods' include those goods specified as dangerous by the British Railways Board (BRB) classification and goods which, although not included in this classification, 'are of a similar kind'. Without such a blanket definition of dangerous goods, however imprecise, the conditions would have become unbalanced, with the need to include highly technical classifications of dangerous goods more appropriate to the shipping industry.

Parties and subcontracting (Condition 2)

To reflect the significance of subcontracting in the haulage industry, the RHA conditions have this to say:

1. The Trader warrants that he is either the owner of the goods in any Consignment or is authorized by such owner to accept these Conditions on such owner's behalf.
2. The Carrier and any other carrier employed by the Carrier may employ the services of any other carrier for the purpose of fulfilling the Contract in whole or in part and the name of every such other carrier shall be provided to the Trader on request.
3. The Carrier contracts for itself and as agent of and trustee for its servants and agents and all other carriers referred to in (2) above and such other carrier's servants and agents and every reference in Conditions 3–17

inclusive hereof to 'The Carrier' shall be deemed to include every such other carrier, servant and agent with the intention that they shall have the benefit of the Contract and collectively and together with the Carrier be under no greater liability to the Trader or any other party than is the Carrier hereunder.

As the carrier, you are thus obliged to notify your customer, the trader, if you propose to use subcontract haulage. Remember, that as the carrier, you remain legally responsible for the actions of your subcontract haulier. Therefore, the terms of any subcontract should be very carefully drafted.

The terms plainly state that the carrier has contractual remedies against a subcontractor, provided that the subcontract haulier is made aware by the carrier that the subcontract is subject to the 1982 RHA Conditions of Carriage.

Dangerous goods (Condition 3)

If the Carrier agrees to accept Dangerous Goods for carriage such goods must be accompanied by a full declaration of their nature and contents and be properly and safely packed and labelled in accordance with any statutory regulations for the time being in force for carriage by road.

A new set of statutory regulations on the classification, labelling and packaging of dangerous goods came into force on 1 January 1986. (For a commentary on these regulations, see A Manager's Guide to International Road Freighting.) For the haulier seriously contemplating the carriage of dangerous goods, the FTA, for example, runs excellent practical training courses designed to give the inexperienced carrier of such goods a proper understanding of the complex rules and regulations on this subject.

Beware the occasional haulage of dangerous goods (to make up a full load, for instance). Unless you specialize in this form of road transport, you are likely to fall outside the strict confines of statutory regulations. This is a legal minefield, and infringement of the regulations can lead to severe penalties, both civil and criminal.

Loading and unloading (Condition 4)

Condition 4 makes it clear that in usual circumstances the carrier will not provide additional facilities such as mechanical loading and unloading devices; these facilities are the customer's responsibility.

Consignment notes (Condition 5)

This condition provides that a consignment note can act as a receipt but under contract law should not be taken as 'evidence of the condition or of the correctness of the declared nature, quantity, or weight of the Consignment at the time it is received by the Carrier'.

It has to be remembered that in the case of a unitized load, whether palletized or containerized, the driver cannot be expected to pontificate upon the true nature, condition or quality of the goods being carried.

Transit (Condition 6)

1. Transit shall commence when the Carrier takes possession of the Consignment whether at the point of collection or at the Carrier's premises.
2. Transit shall (unless otherwise previously determined) end when the Consignment is tendered at the usual place of delivery at the consignee's address within the customary carriage hours of the district. Provided that:
   (a) If no safe and adequate access or no adequate unloading facilities there exist then transit shall be deemed to end at the expiry of one clear day after notice in writing (or by telephone if so previously agreed in writing) of the arrival of the Consignment at the Carrier's premises has been sent to the consignee; and
   (b) when for any other reason whatever a Consignment cannot be delivered or when a Consignment is held by the Carrier 'to await order' or 'to be kept till called for' or upon any like instructions and such instructions are not given or the Consignment is not called for and removed, within a reasonable time, then transit shall be deemed to end.

As a matter of prudent practice, it is a good idea to obtain a standard international operator's licence as well as a domestic one. An international journey is simply one involving a foreign element. The movement of trailers destined for foreign locations to or from port terminals in the United Kingdom may be carried out under a standard (domestic) licence. However, operating under cover of a domestic licence does seem rather restrictive in today's international business environment.

Undelivered or unclaimed goods (Condition 7)

Undelivered or unclaimed goods may be sold by the carrier in certain circumstances. This is an exceedingly technical provision. The carrier who, after making reasonable enquiries on the matter, wishes to sell the goods, should consider taking legal advice before putting in hand the sale. If the sale is not carried out properly, that is in accordance with the provisions of Condition 7, the carrier will be liable for any loss or damage arising.

Carrier's charges (Condition 8)

The important subject of carrier's charges is covered by Condition 8 which provides:

1. The Carrier's charges shall be payable by the Trader without prejudice to the Carrier's rights against the consignee or any other person. Provided that when goods are consigned 'carriage forward' the Trader shall not be required to pay such charges unless the consignee fails to pay after a reasonable demand has been made by the carrier for payment thereof.
2. Except where a quotation states otherwise, all quotations based on a tonnage rate shall apply to the gross weight unless:
    (a) the goods exceed 2.25 cubic metres in measurement per tonne, in which case the tonnage rate shall be computed upon and apply to each measurement of 2.25 cubic metres or any part thereof, or
    (b) The size or shape of a Consignment necessitates the use of a vehicle of greater carrying capacity than the weight of the Consignment would otherwise

require, in which case the tonnage rate shall be computed upon and apply to the carrying capacity of such vehicle as is reasonably required.

3. Charges shall be payable on the expiry of any time limit previously stipulated and the carrier shall be entitled to interest at the average of the overdraft interest rates being charged at Lloyds Bank plc and Barclays Bank plc current at this time, calculated on a daily basis on all amounts overdue to the carrier.

Liability for loss and damage (Condition 9)

1. The Trader shall be deemed to have elected to accept the terms set out in (2) of this Condition unless, before the transit commences, the Trader has agreed in writing that the Carrier shall not be liable for any loss or misdelivery of or damage to goods however or whenever caused and whether or not caused or contributed to directly or indirectly by any act, omission, neglect, default or other wrongdoing on the part of the Carrier.

2. Subject to these Conditions the Carrier shall be liable for:
    (i) loss or misdelivery of or damage to livestock, bullion, money, securities, stamps, precious metals or precious stones only if
    (a) the Carrier has specifically agreed in writing to carry any such items and
    (b) the Trader has agreed in writing to reimburse the Carrier in respect of all additional costs which result from the carrying of the said items and
    (c) the loss, misdelivery or damage is occasioned during transit and results from negligent act or omission by the Carrier;
    (ii) any loss or misdelivery of or damage to any other goods occasioned during transit unless the same has arisen from, and the Carrier has used reasonable care to minimize the effects of
    (a) act of God;
    (b) any consequences of war, invasion, act of foreign enemy, hostilities (whether war or not), civil war, rebellion, insurrection, military or usurped power

or confiscation, requisition, or destruction of or damage to property by or under the order of any government or public or local authority;

(c) seizure or forfeiture under legal process;

(d) error, act, omission, mis-statement or misrepresentation by the Trader or other owner of the goods or by servants or agents of either of them;

(e) inherent liability to wastage in bulk or weight, latent defect or inherent defect, vice or natural deterioration of the goods;

(f) insufficient or improper packing;

(g) insufficient or improper labelling or addressing;

(h) riot, civil commotion, strike, lockout, general or partial stoppage or restraint of labour from whatever cause;

(j) consignee not taking or accepting delivery within a reasonable time after the Consignment has been tendered.

3. The Carrier shall not in any circumstances be liable for loss of or damage to goods after transit of such goods is deemed to have ended within the meaning of Condition 6(2) hereof, whether or not caused or contributed to directly or indirectly by any act, omission, neglect, default or other wrongdoing on the part of the Carrier.

The object of Condition 9, encouraged by the Office of Fair Trading, is to allow the trader to make his own insurance arrangements to cover the risks of loss and damage to goods.

Fraud (Condition 10)

The general rule excludes the carrier from liability for fraud on the part of the trader 'or the owner of the goods or the servants or agents of either in respect of that consignment'. However, if the carrier or an employee in the course of his employment act as accomplices in a fraud, they are liable. The following case provides a very good illustration of the legal problems arising from allegations of fraud.

In *Faccenda Chicken Ltd v Fowler and Others*, Fowler v Faccenda Chicken Ltd (1986 1 All ER 617) the scope of an employee's duty to his former employer came before the Court of Appeal. In 1973 Faccenda Chicken Ltd (the company) employed Mr Fowler as its sales manager. At his own suggestion, he sold fresh chicken from refrigerated vans which travelled through particular routes within a defined area in the Midlands.

Under Mr Fowler's van sales operation, ten refrigerated vehicles travelled in certain sectors, radiating from the company's factory at Brackley in Northamptonshire, offering fresh chickens to traders like butchers, supermarkets and caterers. The whole operation was based on 50 journeys or rounds, one for each vehicle on every working day of the week. By 1980 the operation was clearly prospering, bringing in on average £2500 per week in the second half of the year. Unfortunately, on 11 December 1980 Mr Fowler was arrested with another on a charge of stealing some chickens from his employer (in fact he was acquitted of the charge at his trial in September 1981). He resigned as sales manager and the following year had a similar van sales operation of his own, using eight former employees of the company.

On 10 September 1981 (the date of his acquittal!), an action was brought by the company against Mr Fowler and the eight former employees alleging an unlawful conspiracy and breach of implied terms of contract that they would faithfully serve Faccenda Chicken Ltd and 'would not use confidential information and/or trade secrets gained by them and each of them whilst in the company's employment to the disadvantage or detriment of the company, whether during the currency of such employment or after its cessation'.

Incidentally, for his part, on 16 September 1982 Mr Fowler issued a writ in the High Court claiming almost £23,000 for arrears of commission owed to him by the company.

The main case put by the company was that the new Fowler van sales operation had wrongfully used confidential information obtained during employment with the company.

This sales information comprised:

- customers' names and addresses
- the best routes to take to reach individual customers
- details of quantity and quality needs of customers
- good times of the day and days of the week to make deliveries to individual customers
- prices acceptable to customers.

This information allegedly comprised a package which

amounted to confidential information.

At first instance the judge dismissed both claims. The new Fowler operation had certainly made use of the sales information, but this did not involve any breach of contract by Mr Fowler and the other former employees, nor did it shows an actionable conspiracy. On appeal by the company, it was held that the duty of fidelity owed by Fowler and others to the company as former employees was not as great as that owed by an employee during the course of his employment.

In this case, as the sales information was neither a trade secret nor could be regarded as so confidential that it needed the same protection as a trade secret, the appeal failed. The Court of Appeal made it clear that an employer could not use a restrictive covenant in an employment contract to protect confidential information unless that information could be classified as a trade secret or equivalent. (Tests to determine the existence of a trade secret were naturally discussed in this case.)

It should be noted that an employee will be in breach of his duty of good faith owed to his employer while employed by him if he makes, copies or deliberately memorizes a list of his employer's customers for use after leaving this employment. This is very difficult to prove in practice! Furthermore, there is no general rule of law preventing a former employee canvassing or doing business with customers of his former employer. However unsatisfactory this may appear to the haulier wishing to protect his business, this is the state of the law.

Limitation of Liability (Condition 11)

1. Except as otherwise provided in these Conditions the liability of the Carrier in respect of loss or misdelivery of or damage to goods shall in all circumstances be limited as follows:

    (a) where loss, misdelivery or damage, however sustained, is in respect of the whole of the Consignment, to a sum calculated at the rate of £800 per tonne on either the gross weight of the Consignment or, where applicable, the tonnage computed in accordance with Condition 8(2)(a) or (b) hereof:

(b) where loss, misdelivery or damage, however sustained, is in respect of part of the Consignment, to the proportion of the sum ascertained in accordance with (1)(a) of this Condition which the actual value of that part of the Consignment bears to the actual value of the whole of the Consignment.

Provided that:

(i) nothing in this Condition shall limit the liability of the Carrier to less than the sum of £10;

(ii) the Carrier shall be entitled to require proof of the value of the whole of the Consignment and of any part thereof lost, misdelivered or damaged;

(iii) the Trader shall be entitled at any time prior to commencement of transit to give seven days' written notice to the Carrier requiring that the aforementioned £800 per tonne limit be increased but not so as to exceed the value of the Consignment and in the event of such notice being given the Trader shall within the said seven days agree with the Carrier an increase in the carriage charges in consideration of the said increased limit.

2. Notwithstanding condition 11(1), the liability of the Carrier in respect of the indirect or consequential loss or damage, however arising and including loss of market, shall not exceed the amount of the carriage charges in respect of the Consignment or the amount of the claimant's proved loss, whichever is the smaller, unless:

(a) at the time of entering into the Contract with the Carrier the Trader declares to the Carrier a special interest in delivery in the case of loss or damage or of an agreed time limit being exceeded and agrees to pay a surcharge calculated on the amount of that interest, and

(b) prior to the commencement of transit the Trader has delivered to the Carrier written confirmation of the special interest, agreed time limit and amount of the interest.

Limitation on liability is placed at £800 per tonne which should be monitored and adjusted in the case of higher value consignments.

As Condition 11(2) extends the liability of the carrier to indirect or consequential loss or damage, including loss of market, suitable goods in transit cover should be taken out to cover this area of risk.

Indemnity to the carrier (Condition 12)

The Trader shall indemnify the Carrier against:

1. all consequences suffered by the Carrier (including but not limited to claims, demands, proceedings, fines, penalties, damages, costs, expenses, and loss of or damage to the carrying vehicle and to other goods carried) of any error, omission, mis-statement or misrepresentation by the Trader or other owner of the goods or by any servant or agent of either of them, insufficient or improper packing, labelling or addressing of the goods or fraud as in Condition 10:
2. all claims and demands whatever by whoever made in excess of the liability of the Carrier under these Conditions:
3. all losses suffered by and claims made against the Carrier in consequence of loss of or damage to property caused by or arising out of the carriage by the Carrier of Dangerous Goods whether or not declared by the Trader as such:
4. all claims made upon the Carrier by HM Customs and Excise in respect of dutiable goods consigned in bond whether or not transit has ended or been suspended.

Naturally, the carrier cannot be held responsible for loss or damage which results from the trader's carelessness or negligence. Accordingly, Condition 12 requires the trader to indemnify the carrier in this regard.

Time limits for claims (Condition 13)

Condition 13 makes it clear that a claim brought against the carrier by the customer is subject to strict time limits; in the case of loss from or damage to a package, the customer must advise the carrier of his claim in writing within three days and the claim must be made within seven days. In the case of non-delivery, wrong delivery or loss of a consignment or of any separate package, the respective time limits for advising and making the claim are 28 days and 42 days.

General lien (Condition 14)

The Carrier shall have a general lien against the owner of the goods for any monies whatever due from the Trader or such other owner to the Carrier. If any such lien is not satisfied within a reasonable time the Carrier may at his absolute discretion sell the goods, or part thereof, as agent for the owner and apply the proceeds towards the monies due and the expenses of the retention, insurance and sale of the goods and shall, upon accounting to the Trader for any balance remaining, be discharged from all liability whatever in respect of the goods.

There is a great deal of misunderstanding about the operation of a lien, general or special, under English law. A power of sale under a general lien should not normally be exercised without recourse to legal advice. Given the carrier's obligation to obtain the best possible price for the goods to be sold, good advice on what constitutes such a price in prevailing market conditions must surely be taken.

As a matter of interest, the following definition of general lien appears in Mozley & Whiteley's Law Dictionary:

The right of a bailee to detain a chattel from its owner until payment be made, not only in respect of that particular article, but of any balance that may be due, on a general account between the bailor and bailee in the same line of business.

Unreasonable detention (Condition 15)

This condition is self-explanatory.

The Trader shall be liable for the cost of unreasonable detention of any vehicle, trailer, container or sheet but the rights of the Carrier against any other person in respect thereof shall remain unaffected.

Computation of time (Condition 16)

When calculating the time limits laid down by the RHA conditions, certain days have to be excluded. If a time limit is seven days or less, public holidays, Saturdays and Sundays do not count.

Impossibility of performance (Condition 17)

Naturally, there are occasions when it is not possible for the carrier to deliver the goods.

> The Carrier shall be relieved of its obligation to perform the contract to the extent that the performance thereof is prevented by failure of the Trader, fire, weather conditions, industrial dispute, labour disturbance or cause beyond the reasonable control of the Carrier.

Careful consideration should be given to the likely practical meaning of such 'get-outs' as 'industrial dispute'. Does it makes any difference, for example, whether the dispute is official or unofficial? In the current political climate, an official strike would count under Condition 17 but not an unofficial one.

Overdrive contract

To cope with the peaks and troughs of road transport operation, the busy haulier will need to consider hiring in outside drivers. The specialist hiring firm, Overdrive, has a standard form contract which sets out the contractual relationship between the haulier, Overdrive and the Overdrive driver. This contract, which is reproduced here, is a typical example of a standard form contract found in the haulage industry.

In Overdrive's 'Terms and Conditions of Business for Driving', Overdrive is referred to as 'the company' and the haulier hiring an Overdrive driver, 'the client'. In the following comments we refer to 'Overdrive' and the 'haulier'.

Clause 1 confirms that drivers hired from Overdrive become the temporary employees of the haulier and are under the complete control of the haulier. The driver must obey lawful instructions on what he does and also on 'the manner of his doing it'.

Clause 2 gives the haulier a reasonable 'get out'. If the driver provided by Overdrive proves unsuitable (no doubt an unusual occurrence in practice) the haulier need not engage him provided reasonable notice is given of this intention to Overdrive.

Clause 3 imposes a number of obligations on Overdrive,

OVERDRIVE

Terms and Conditions
of Business for Driving (8.79)

These Terms and Conditions as stated overleaf
set out the contractual relationship between
Overdrive, our Client and the Overdrive
driver. It defines Overdrive's responsibilities
in providing drivers, together with the benefit
of the indemnities and guarantees which we offer.
It also sets out the obligations of our Client in
respect of Operator's Licences and
other Road Traffic Enactments.

The terms on which drivers of motorised vehicles are seconded

Between . . . . ("the Company")

and . . . . ("the Client")

are as follows:

CONTRACTS

Terms and Conditions of Business for Driving (8.79)

1. Drivers are employed by the Company for the purpose of supplying those drivers to Clients. Subject to Clauses 2 and 8 hereof, on introduction to the Client and for so long as their secondment continues, drivers become the temporary servants of the Client employed by it to drive its vehicles for its own use, on the terms agreed with the drivers by the Company, such terms to be notified to the Client at the commencement of the secondment. In particular, but without prejudice to the generality of the foregoing, the Client shall have entire and absolute control over the driver, both in what he does and the manner of his doing it.

2. If, when the driver first reports for duty with the Client, the Client considers him unsuitable, the Client may decline to accept the driver and in such event, if the Client gives notice to that effect to the Company by telephone and confirms in writing as soon as practicable and at the latest within 24 hours from the time the driver first reports for duty, the Client will not be liable to make any payment to the Company for its services in respect of that driver and provided always that the Company shall not be liable for any loss or damage whatsoever, caused by the Client declining to engage a particular driver, or by the Company's failure to provide a substitute for that driver.

3. The Company will perform or has performed and the Client will accept the following services in respect of the driver:
    (a) On behalf of the Client checking the relevant qualifications and licences of such drivers and taking up their references.
    (b) Paying to the drivers the wages, overtime, holiday pay, and other emoluments to which they are entitled under their contracts with the Company.
    (c) Paying Employers' National Insurance Contributions and maintaining employer's liability insurance in respect of the drivers' employment.
    (d) Making all necessary and proper deductions from the wages, overtime and other emoluments of the driver for National Insurance Contributions and any direct taxation required to be deducted from such emoluments.
    (e) Accounting to the Inland Revenue or other appropriate bodies for all such deductions as are mentioned in (b) above.
    (f) Making and keeping all necessary records relating to the matters specified in (a) to (e) above.
    (g) Giving to the driver written particulars of terms of employment pursuant to the Employment Protection (Consolidation) Act, 1978, and in accordance with other enactments relating thereto.
    (h) Whether on behalf of the Company or the Client, dealing with applications for the redress of any grievance of the driver concerning his secondment to the Client.

4. The Company will ensure that all drivers it may introduce to the Client in pursuance of this agreement are, at the commencement of their secondment to the Client, duly qualified and licensed, in accordance with the provisions of the Road Traffic Act, 1972, and any other enactment relating thereto, and such rules and regulations made thereunder or under any other Statute relating to the same which may, from time to time, be enforced to drive vehicles falling within such groups or classes of vehicles as the Client may specify to the Company prior to the time that any such driver first reports for work.

5. Except as provided in Clause 3 the Client himself takes direct responsibility for all employer's obligations arising from the temporary secondment of the driver to him including, without prejudice to the generality of this provision, all statutory duties in respect of driving licences, operator's licences, driver's hours and records, maintenance and safety of vehicles and Road Traffic and other liability insurances Health and Safety Regulations including, but not limited to, fully comprehensive insurance for his vehicles and their contents.

6. The Client will make payment to the Company in accordance with the scale current from time to time during the secondment of the driver and notified by the Company to the Client in writing and/or orally.

7. Payments are due within 7 days of the date of invoice.

8. The Client may at any time terminate the secondment of a driver provided that: Except in cases involving gross misconduct, or failure to devote such time and attention as may be required properly to carry out his duties, the Client gives the required notice to the Company as set out in the Work Specification issued by the Company.

Terms and Conditions of Business for Driving (8.79) Continued

9.   The Company shall not be liable for any loss or damage whatsoever caused by the absence of the driver or by cessation of the driver's secondment. Although the Company will, if requested, attempt to find a replacement driver, it does not guarantee to do so, and is not liable for any loss or damage whatsoever resulting from its failure to do so.

10.   The Company reserves the right to sub-contract the provision of drivers to Overdrive Limited to licensees of Overdrive Limited or to their subsidiaries (as appropriate), and such sub-contractor or sub-contractors shall for the purposes of the performance of this contract be in the same position as the Company.

11.   Exemption Clause and Right to Indemnify

The Company will indemnify the Client in respect of any direct pecuniary loss sustained by the Client which is caused by an act or acts of fraud or dishonesty on the part of a driver or drivers seconded by the Company pursuant to these terms and conditions, provided that:

(a)   Immediate notice is given by the Client to the Company of any circumstances likely to give rise to a claim pursuant to this provision.

(b)   Save in the case of prior written agreement between the company and the Client, the Company's liability pursuant to this clause shall not exceed the sum of £10,000 in relation to any one driver.

(c)   The Company shall not be liable under this clause for loss of cash, bank currency, promissory notes, securities for money, deeds, bonds, bills of exchange, stamps, medals, coins, jewellery, furs, gold, silver or precious metals, gems, precious stones or articles composed of any of them.

SUBJECT AS AFORESAID it is understood and agreed that:

(i)   Only the Client is in a position to assess and therefore to insure against risks in respect of or arising during the secondment of a driver or drivers to be supplied by the Company, and the Client is obliged to insure against any loss or damage, injury, liability, or expense caused by the driver or drivers or in any way resulting from acts, statements or omissions by him or them howsoever caused.

(ii)   The Company's prices are not calculated upon the basis that it is accepting liability for any such risks.

(iii)   From the moment the driver or drivers first report for duty to the Client the driver or drivers are under the entire and absolute control of the Client; accordingly

A.   The Company shall not be under any liability whatsoever to the Client, its servants or agents, for any loss, expense, damage or delay arising from any failure of drivers to carry out the terms of their employment by the Company or the terms of their secondment to the Client, or in any way arising from acts, statements or omissions of drivers introduced by the Company to the Client howsoever caused save:

(i)   Insofar as such loss, expense, damage or delay is caused or (pro tanto) contributed to by the negligence on the part of the Company its servants or agents in relation to the performance of the obligations set out in Clause 3 hereof provided always that the liability of the Company in any circumstances whatsoever and howsoever arising shall not exceed the amounts paid or payable to the Company by the Client pursuant to Clause 6 hereof.

(ii)   Insofar as such loss, expense, damage or delay is caused or (pro tanto) contributed to by any breach by the Company of its obligations under Clause 4.

(iii)   That it is not intended hereby to exclude or restrict liability for death or personal injury resulting from the Company's negligence or that of its servants or agents.

B.   The Client shall at all times keep the company effectively indemnified against all actions, proceedings, costs, charges, claims, expenses and demands whatsoever which may be made or brought against the Company in respect of any injury, loss damage or expense, howsoever or whensoever caused as a result of or arising out of the supply to the Client by the Company of drivers or any acts, statements or omissions of drivers while seconded to the Client.

C.   The Exclusion Clause and right of indemnity herein shall inure to the benefit not only of the Company, but also its directors, servants or agents.

12.   This contract shall be construed and interpreted in accordance to English law and the parties hereby submit to the jurisdiction of the High Court in London.

Signatory on behalf of Client . . . .

Title . . . .

Date . . . .

Client's Name . . . .

Client's Head Office Address . . . .

. . . .

. . . .

including paying the drivers on hire, accounting for national insurance contributions, making necessary deductions for Inland Revenue purposes and keeping records of payments; it is a welcome relief for the haulier to have these administrative tasks lifted from his shoulders. Indeed, one of the most important selling points put forward by Overdrive is their ability to handle the administrative burden of employing drivers. An important example of Overdrive's administrative function (Clause 3(g)) is the giving of written particulars of employment to a driver. The taking up of a driver's references, checking qualifications and licences are all done by Overdrive.

Clause 4 simply gives more details of this filter system for checking qualifications and licences.

Clause 5 reminds the haulage firm that apart from Overdrive's obligations contained in Clause 3, the haulier must take full responsibility for ensuring that the driver is made aware of such vital matters as drivers' hours and records, maintenance and safety of vehicles. When the rules concerning driver's hours changed significantly on 29 September 1986 the haulier, not Overdrive, had the task of informing all drivers on the new provisions. Similarly, when new Construction and Use Regulations were introduced on 1 August 1986, the haulier had another driver training task to undertake. The advent of the fixed penalty system for all drivers, whether commercial or not, on 1 October 1986 is yet another example of the changing nature of law for the haulier which has had to be notified to employee drivers.

Clause 6 refers to scale payments. The haulier should make quite sure which scale applies in his particular case and not assume it will necessarily be the same as before. Payment should be made within seven days of Overdrive's invoice – a very short period of credit in the haulage industry, it will be noted.

Clause 8 gives the haulier the right to dismiss an Overdrive employee, but is not an easy clause to understand; for instance, what is meant by gross misconduct? In practice, some further explanation of the meaning of this clause should be sought from Overdrive. The question of unfair dismissal figures too often in employment law to leave the operation of Clause 8 to chance.

Clause 9 provides an interesting exemption clause.

Overdrive will try to find a replacement driver but offers no guarantee in this regard. This clause appears perfectly understandable from the viewpoint of a supplier of drivers.

Clause 10 contains a subcontract provision allowing licensees of Overdrive Limited and their subsidiaries, as well as the company itself, actually to supply drivers. Again, from the supplier's standpoint, a necessary provision.

Clause 11, 'Exemption Clause and Right to Indemnify', is emphasized in heavy type because it limits the liability of Overdrive to the haulier in certain specified circumstances. If a driver supplied by Overdrive commits an act of dishonesty or fraud, Overdrive offers a limited form of indemnity to the haulier for loss or damage suffered. Immediate notice must be given of a likely claim against Overdrive. Usually, the limit of indemnity is set at £10,000. No indemnity will be given for loss of cash, bank currency and so on listed in Clause 11(c) – a substantial limitation of liability.

The SUBJECT AS AFORESAID proviso reminds the haulier that Overdrive's rates are not based on accepting liability for matters which the prudent haulier should insure against. Given the driver supplied by Overdrive is 'under the entire and absolute control' of the haulier, adequate insurance cover needs to be arranged by the haulier to cover wrongful acts or omissions by a driver. Accordingly, a copy of this clause should be given to one's insurance broker to make sure sufficient insurance cover is taken out. Clause 11(b) is so far-ranging that an alert professional insurance adviser would probably need some explanation of the likely liability of the haulier 'howsoever or whensoever caused as a result of or arising out of the supply to the client by the company of drivers'.

Clause 12 underlines the fairly obvious point that the contract made between Overdrive and the haulier is subject to English law. English law has included Community law since the UK joined the European Economic Community in 1973.

It will be understood from this brief commentary that in standard form contracts the haulier should remain on his guard and not be afraid to seek professional advice, especially on insurance matters, before making a contractual commitment to a document which, naturally, affords wide protection to the contracting party responsible for drawing it up and seeks to limit the scope of protection afforded by law for the other party.

Validity of haulage contracts

Whether a contract is of a standard type or a 'one-off', it must contain certain elements, otherwise it cannot be enforced in the courts. The haulier and the other contracting party must want to be bound contractually by their promises. In business the legal presumption is that the parties do intend to make a valid contract. However, this presumption can be rebutted in particular cases where it can be shown that, even in a business situation, the parties do not in fact want to make an enforceable contract. In social or domestic arrangements, on the other hand, the legal presumption is that the person making the promise and the party receiving the benefit do not intend to create legal relations. Again, this presumption can be rebutted by evidence showing a contrary intention viz. the parties did want to make an enforceable contract, notwithstanding the domestic or social environment.

The parties must have a legal capacity to contract. In the business world it is sensible to enquire if the person you are dealing with does in fact have the authority to make a contract on behalf of his firm. It is surprising how often this proves not to be the case. As far as age is concerned, a person who has reached 18 has the legal capacity to contract as an individual. (Special rules apply to the ability of a minor to contract.)

Given an intention to make a business agreement enforceable in the courts and the necessary legal capacity, the parties must show a valid offer and acceptance have been made. For detailed discussion of the distinction between an offer and an invitation to treat readers should turn to standard law textbooks and refer to such cases as Fisher v Bell (1961) and Pharmaceutical Society of Great Britain v Boots Cash Chemists (Southern) Ltd (1953).

For the purpose of making a haulage contract, an offer may call for acceptance of the haulage services on offer by another promise or by conduct. In the first case the haulier and the other party undertake to carry out certain obligations (typically the haulage of goods for an agreed price) and the contract is made by exchange of these promises. In the alternative case the offer is simply accepted by performance.

It should be remembered that an offer may be withdrawn any time before acceptance, unless the person making the offer receives something of value to keep the offer open or the offer is made under seal.

Assuming an offer has been accepted in unqualified terms (a counter-offer for example is tantamount to a rejection of the original offer), a valid contract must show each contracting party will receive some benefit, in money or money's worth – in technical terms, 'consideration'. The common law doctrine of consideration, unknown to countries on the European mainland, is best left to lawyers' discussion. In haulage contracts there will be little doubt as to whether each party has received a worthwhile benefit!

Some contracts, such as hire purchase contracts and contracts for the sale and purchase of land, need to be in a special form. Haulage contracts do not even need to be in writing. An oral contract for supplying a haulage service is just as enforceable as a written one for this purpose. Of course, it is much better to have a written contract, because proving a contract relying on the spoken word can be notoriously difficult.

When making a contract be sure that you are both talking about the same thing. Are you, the haulier, agreeing, for example, to supply a particular vehicle for haulage or to supply any lorry which happens to be available at the time the contract needs to be undertaken? In short, there has to be no room for misunderstanding; there must be what lawyers call consensus ad idem or a meeting of minds. This point may sound very obvious, but it is seen to be crucial when one party to the contract is looking for a way to get out of his contractual obligations and is able to seize upon an ill-defined point.

To be enforced in the courts a contract must not be illegal. The mass of legislation governing the haulage industry makes it quite easy to step outside the confines of the law, albeit inadvertently. So special attention should be given to any unusual contract terms you may be called upon to agree to in case these make the contract illegal.

According to Professor Roy Goode, a contract is affected by illegality if:

(a) the making of the contract is unlawful; or
(b) the promise or consideration stipulated is the performance of an unlawful act; or
(c) though the contract is not in itself unlawful, the purpose for which it is made or for which the subject matter is to be applied is unlawful or the intended method of performance is unlawful; or
(d) though free from any of the above defects, the contract stems from or is collateral to another agreement affected by illegality.

Thus, the general law of contract governing the formation of a valid haulage contract has these requirements:

- there must be an intention to create legal relations
- the parties must have capacity to contract
- there must be offer and acceptance
- there must be consideration
- no special form is needed
- consensus ad idem
- there must be no illegality.

Remedies for breach of contract

Assuming a valid haulage contract has been made and one party is in breach of one or more of the terms, the usual remedy is to sue the party in default for damages. The three rules relating to the award of damages for breach of contract were underlined in the famous Victoria Laundry (Windsor) Ltd v Newman Industrial Ltd (1949) case:

1. Damages are awarded by way of compensation to the plaintiff for the loss suffered.
2. Damages only follow when the loss arises naturally from the breach and might have been anticipated by the parties.
3. The plaintiff must attempt to minimize the loss arising from the breach, referred to as a 'duty to mitigate your loss'.

If a major term of the agreement, going to the heart of the contract, is breached, this term, called a condition, allows a plaintiff to repudiate the contract. When a minor term of the contract, called a warranty, is breached, the plaintiff may not repudiate the contract but only sue for damages; breach of a warranty is said to sound in damages only.

Courts have a discretion, in special circumstances, to award an alternative remedy to damages for breach of contract. Where damages are clearly not an adequate remedy, an order for specific performance may be granted. This order compels a person to do something under a contract which he or she has refused to do. It is rarely granted in commercial disputes. An injunction, on the other hand, is becoming increasingly popular as an effective remedy for breach of contract. An injunction is an order directing someone not to do something.

In 1986 the tactics used by Mr Rupert Murdoch to make sure that his newspapers were taken from 'Fortress Wapping' to delivery points throughout the country were very much in the news. In order to maintain effective distribution movements, the TNT lorries carrying the newspapers had the benefit of injunctions forbidding pickets to interfere with their lawful progress. Attempts to breach these injunctions resulted in severe financial penalties being imposed on the print unions and the eventual cessation of hostilities.

A remedy for damages is mandatory for breach of contract, but an injunction is dependent on the court's discretion.

Exclusion clauses

There are several examples of exclusion clauses, often called exemption clauses, in this and other chapters. The haulier will seek to exclude his contractual liability for certain acts or omissions, just like any other shrewd businessman. However, there is some limit to the extent to which a person may seek to contract out of his liability under English law. Clauses seeking to exclude liability, especially in standard form contracts, have come under strong attack from the judges in recent years. The freedom to limit liability was curtailed by the Unfair Contract Terms Act 1977. This affects all contracts with exclusion clauses. So when making haulage contracts, the 1977 Act cannot be ignored.

Chapter 3
Operator Licensing

The subject of operator licensing is at the heart of the law governing the activities of all hauliers. You cannot proceed in business without a licence, and the licensing authority (LA) can revoke a licence if its terms are not strictly complied with. Using a vehicle in contravention of the relevant statutory provisions constitutes a criminal offence.

Use of a goods vehicle

The general rule is that no one may use a goods vehicle on a road for the carriage of goods for hire or reward, or for or in connexion with any trade or business carried on by him, except under an operator's licence (commonly known as an O licence). It is the haulier who must hold the licence.

Some definitions

The *user* of the vehicle is the owner of the vehicle or the person in whose possession it is under some hiring or leasing agreement; this is often not the driver himself but the driver's employer or principal. (Case 1 described in the casenotes at the end of this chapter is relevant here.)

A *goods vehicle* is a motor vehicle constructed or adapted for use for the carriage of goods or a trailer which is so constructed or adapted.

A *road* is described in the Road Traffic Act 1972 as any highway and any other road to which the public has access, including bridges over which a road passes. (There is, rather confusingly, more than one definition of a road in transport legislation.)

The *carriage of goods for hire or reward* occurs when the owner or user of the goods vehicle obtains a tangible benefit in money or money's worth. This benefit can be direct or indirect and is sometimes referred to by lawyers as 'consideration'.

Exemptions

Various categories of vehicle are exempt from the need to obtain an operating licence. The most significant is the *small goods vehicle*. This is defined as a goods vehicle which does not form part of a vehicle combination and has a relevant plated weight not exceeding 3500kg, or (not having a plated weight) has an unladen weight not exceeding 1525kg.

If a *trailer* can carry goods (a piece of mobile plant obviously cannot) it must be taken into account if over 1020kg unladen weight.

No licence is needed for a *motor vehicle and drawbar trailer combination* if the gross plated weights do not exceed 3500kg, or, if unplated, the total unladen weights do not exceed 1525kg. Similar exemptions are granted to articulated tractor and semi-trailer combinations.

Exemption is also given to certain *specialized vehicles*, including: public service vehicles, hackney carriages, police vehicles, fire engines, ambulances, vehicles being used with trade plates, local authority vehicles used for road cleansing and the collection or disposal of refuse, vehicles used solely on airports, showmen's goods vehicles and their trailers.

Transfer of an O licence

An O licence cannot usually be transferred to another person, but in the event of the death, incapacity, bankruptcy or liquidation of the holder of a licence, a special procedure may be followed. The survivor in the haulage business is deemed to be the licence holder if within two months he notifies the licensing authority of the event and within four months applies for a new O licence. In the case of a restricted O licence the survivor must make application within two months for a new licence.

Types of O licence

The three types of O licence available are: restricted, standard and standard (international).

The *restricted licence* covers domestic and international goods vehicle operation for own account haulage. The term 'own account' includes (in the words of the FTA) 'the delivery and collection of goods sold, bought, used or let on hire or hire purchase or processed in the course of the operator's trade or business whether transport costs are included in the price of the articles involved or charged separately'. The carriage of goods for a subsidiary or for a holding company and for other companies which are subsidiaries of the same holding company is generally regarded as own account for these purposes.

The *standard O licence* allows the haulier to carry goods for hire or reward in the UK and to operate on an own account basis domestically and internationally.

Standard (international) permits give hauliers the freedom to operate either hire and reward or own account at home and abroad.

Obtaining an O licence

A haulier wishing to commence goods vehicle operations needing an O licence must apply for one at least nine weeks beforehand to give the licensing authority enough time to make enquiries as to the haulier's suitability to hold such a licence.

Application forms

The main form of application which the haulier must complete is known as a GV 79. This form covers: the type of O licence needed, haulier's status, previous experience, relevant convictions (if any), financial position, maintenance arrangements for vehicles, details of nominated transport managers (not needed for restricted O licence), particulars of advertisement of application, a list of vehicles and their location at proposed operating centres, plus a declaration by the haulier that he will abide by the rules of the O licensing system. Another form, GV 79A, gives further details of the proposed goods vehicle operation and is filed in support of the main form of application.

Advertisement of application

The main purpose of advertising the application for an O licence is to give local residents and other interested parties an opportunity to raise any objections to or comments on the proposed licence. The advertisement is in a prescribed format and a typical example of an advertisement in a local newspaper is shown below.

Specimen advertisement Application for O licence

GOODS VEHICLES OPERATOR'S LICENCE

Notice of Application for Grant

Swannson-on-Wheels, whose address is: Delderfield Close, The Kentish Hexagon, near Westerham, Kent, is applying for an Operator's licence under which the land referred to below will be used as an operating centre for five vehicles and three trailers. The said land is Unit 7, Medway Trading Estate, near Chatham, Kent. Any person who is entitled to and wishes to make representations against the grant of the application on environmental grounds may make written representation to the Licensing Authority at the Traffic Area Office at Ivy House, 3 Ivy Terrace, Eastbourne, BN21 4QT within 21 days of the date on which this notice is published.

Further information about the application and any entitlement to make representations may be obtained from that Traffic Area Office. A copy of the representations must be sent to Swannson-on-Wheels at the address given.

Objections and Representations

Certain organizations have the power to object to the grant of an O licence and it is important for the haulier seeking a licence to be aware of who they are:

- local authorities
- police authorities

- planning authorities
- trade associations:
  British Association of Removers
  Freight Transport Association
  Road Haulage Association
- trade unions:
  General & Municipal Worker's Union
  National Union of Railwaymen
  Transport & General Workers' Union
  Union of Shop Distributive & Allied Workers
  United Road Transport Union.

Local residents can make representations against the grant of a licence on the basis that the proposed operating centre is unsuitable on environmental grounds. Local people making representations have to show that the haulier's operating centre would reduce the enjoyment of their land. A residents' association, parish or town council is not allowed to make representations on behalf of local residents unless it actually owns or occupies land in the vicinity of the proposed operating centre.

Whereas an objector has a right of appeal to the Transport Tribunal against an unfavourable decision of a licensing authority, the local resident has no such right of appeal. Nonetheless, the rights of local residents have to be given very careful consideration by the haulier applying for the grant of an O licence.

The LA's decision

The licensing authority (LA) considers the haulier's application, any representations and objections. The application may be refused, granted or granted subject to limitations.

The applicant must meet clearly defined criteria relating to general fitness, good repute, maintenance arrangements, drivers' hours and overloading, suitability of the operating centre, financial resources and professional competence.

General fitness and good repute

In deciding whether an applicant passes the general fitness tests, the LA will take account of any convictions concerning the operation of goods vehicles over the previous five years. Speeding, drivers' hours and records offences, overloading, keeping an unroadworthy vehicle, forgery, unlawfully using a vehicle, even contravention of parking restrictions and prohibitions, all count against a haulier seeking an O licence, and this is not an exhaustive list. In determining whether a haulier is of good repute, the LA looks at the applicant's conduct generally, not just at any previous convictions he may have.

Maintenance, drivers' hours, records and overloading

There is no question that proper maintenance of goods vehicles lies at the heart of the licensing system. The LA must be satisfied that the applicant will keep vehicles in a good and serviceable condition. Daily running checks need to be made and these checks must be supported by a workable maintenance system. Any defects found have to be rectified without delay. Both driver and staff working at the operating centre need to be fully conversant with effective maintenance procedures.

The LA has to be assured by the applicant that he understands the importance of the rules relating to drivers' hours, records and tachograph requirements, rules which need careful study. Prevention of overloading is another important target for the would-be licence holder.

The operating centre and financial resources

In assessing the suitability of the proposed operating centre, the LA looks at two connected aspects. Most importantly, it must be suitable on environmental grounds; secondly, its suitability must not be prejudiced by a lack of financial resources. Obviously, the LA has to be assured by the applicant that his proposed haulage operations are built on a sound financial foundation. Haulage is particularly prone to cash flow problems. Sufficient working capital must be available to meet the slings and arrows of outrageous misfortune!

There is no statutory definition of 'unsuitability on environmental grounds', and the kind of considerations taken into account by the LA can best be judged by studying actual cases, such as those outlined in the casenotes at the end of this chapter. Although the requirements concerning the environmental suitability of an operating centre have only been in force since June 1984, some interesting cases have already arisen on their interpretation.

The conditions which can be imposed by the LA to reflect environmental considerations are limited to the means of entry and exit for authorized vehicles, times for vehicular access, parking arrangements for vehicles, and the number, type and size of authorized vehicles parked or being maintained at the operating centre.

Professional competence

This subject is important enough to justify a book in its own right. For more detailed information than can be given here, readers should turn to *A Study Manual of Professional Competence in Road Transport Management* by David Lowe.

The LA requires a licence applicant to have sufficient know-how to manage a haulage business in a profitable and law-abiding manner. A glance at the syllabus for the Certificate of Professional Competence (CPC) awarded by the Royal Society of Arts (RSA) in respect of national transport operations shows the area of knowledge required. The CPC national syllabus covers these five main subjects:

- Road safety
- Technical standards and aspects of operation
- Access to the UK market
- Business and financial management
- Law.

The CPC international syllabus is broken down into four main parts:

- Law
- Access to the market
- Customs, practice and formalities
- Operations, technical standards and road safety.

Whereas the CPC national needs 65 hours direct teaching

or equivalent for the 1½-hours examination comprising 60 questions, the CPC international needs 30 hours and has only 30 questions in a one-hour examination. Examinations take place four times a year.

Having passed the CPC national examination an applicant meets the requirement as to professional competence for domestic operations. Naturally the CPC international examination has to be passed before the haulier can embark on international goods vehicle operations with trucks over 3500kg.

There are other ways of meeting the requirement of professional competence. The Chartered Institute of Transport offers a qualification which is increasingly popular for O licence purposes; The Institute of Transport Administration, the Institute of Road Transport Engineers and the Institute of the Furniture Warehousing and Removing Industry all offer qualifications which meet O licence professional competence requirements. Finally, there are 'grandfather's rights' which satisfy the LA requirements: the so-called 'grandfather' produces a Certificate of Competence (GV 203) issued by a LA before 31 December 1979 confirming the holder was in responsible employment in road transport under an operator's licence before 1 January 1975.

If the above criteria are met by the applicant, and any objections or representations prove ill-founded, an O licence is granted on such terms as the LA thinks fit. A licence is usually granted for a period of five years.

Varying the terms of an O licence

An O licence normally authorizes more vehicles to be operated than are listed from the start. Extra vehicles within the margin allowed by the LA can be operated immediately, but the LA has to be notified and a form (GV 80) completed showing the registration numbers and details of the additional vehicles. If the licence does not provide for extra vehicles application for variation of the O licence has to be made on another form (GV 81). If a vehicle needs to be temporarily substituted for one of the operator's authorized vehicles or a vehicle needs to be transferred from one operating centre to another the LA does not need to be informed. An operator wishing to change his type of licence for another type needs to apply for a variation, again using the GV 81. The same procedure applies for a haulier wanting to use a new operating centre.

The FTA Yearbook 1986 has a very useful summary of procedures to adopt when the LA must be notified:

1. If additional vehicles are required to be licensed (Form GV 80 within one month if already authorized, Form GV 81 if not).
2. Of the intention to replace any vehicle (Form GV 80).
3. If a vehicle is no longer operated (Form GV 80 within 21 days).
4. Of the temporary substitution of a vehicle for one off the road if there is no margin (by letter enclosing identity disc of specified vehicle).
5. To use a new operating centre in the same traffic area (Form GV 81).
6. To transfer a vehicle to a new traffic area for more than three months (Form GV 80 old traffic area, Form GV 79, in new area).
7. Of any change in control of the business, its organization of management, or persons holding shares in the company which causes a change in the control of the company (by letter).
8. Of any change in the business name or address (by letter within three weeks. A limited company changing its name will be required to send a copy of the Department of Trade and Industry certificate).
9. Of any change affecting the professional competent person(s) or their position within the company (by letter).
10. Of any event affecting the good repute or professional competence either of the holder of the licence or his nominated transport manager, or the financial standing of the holder of the licence (by letter within 28 days).
11. Following the death, bankruptcy or liquidation of the holder of the licence or the bankruptcy of any of the directors or partners (by letter).

12. Of any changes affecting a company holding a licence involving the acquisition or disposal of subsidiaries (by letter within three weeks accompanied by a GV 80 where appropriate).
13. If an identity disc is lost, destroyed or defaced (immediately by letter).

Enforcement

The LA keeps a watching brief on a haulier's operations under his O licence; the LA must revoke a standard licence if its holder is no longer of good repute, of satisfactory financial standing or professionally competent. In the case of a restricted licence, the LA must revoke it if, twice within a five-year period, the holder is found guilty of carrying goods which should have been covered by a standard or standard international licence.

The LA has the power to revoke, suspend, curtail or prematurely terminate a licence if the holder has (a) broken any conditions attaching to his licence, or (b) been convicted of any offences which are of the type relevant to determination of the applicant's fitness to hold a licence in the first place, or (c) been made bankrupt or gone into liquidation. If the holder's vehicles suffer prohibitions because of unroadworthiness or overloading, if he has made false statements of intent which have not been fulfilled, if there has been a material change of circumstances relating to the licence holder or if an unnominated operating centre has been used, the LA may also revoke, suspend, curtail or prematurely terminate the licence.

Appeal procedure

A LA decision can be appealed against at a Transport Tribunal; applicants for and objectors to a licence also have a right of appeal to the Transport Tribunal against a LA decision.

The London address of the Tribunal is:

Golden Cross House (4th Floor)
Duncannon Street,

London WC2N 4JF
Tel: 01-214 3094

For appeals in Scotland the address is:

Parliament House
Parliament Square
Edinburgh EH1 1RQ
Tel: 031-225 2595

The haulier must lodge his appeal within one month of the LA's decision being formally published. The appeal is heard before a legally qualified chairman and two laymen, both of whom have considerable experience in road transport. In theory an appeal can be handled by the haulier dissatisfied with the LA's decision without the help of professional legal advice and representation before the Tribunal. Indeed, the Consumers' Association have a publication entitled *Taking your own case to court or tribunal* designed to assist the layman wishing to take his own case rather than instruct solicitors; but it warns potential litigants that to take on a particularly complicated legal action without legal help would be madness. It states that not using a lawyer would save you money initially but that it could be a false economy, particularly if your case goes to the High Court, where your opponent will almost certainly have a solicitor and a barrister. Most applicants are represented by a barrister or solicitor specializing in transport law.

An appeal to the Tribunal is made in writing and six copies of the notice of appeal should be sent to Golden Cross House (Parliament House for Scottish appeals). The notice of appeal recites the decision of the LA appealed against, the grounds of appeal and the full names and addresses of every respondent receiving a copy of the appeal. If the appeal is made by an applicant for a licence, the LA and any objectors must, of course, receive a copy. If the appeal is made by an objector, a copy must be sent to the applicant. An administrative fee of £3 is payable by the person lodging the appeal, and a further £3 is payable for each half day devoted to the appeal hearing. These fees are modest, but a person shown to be appealing in a frivolous or vexatious manner may have the costs of the appeal hearing awarded against him. A costs figure for just one day on appeal before the

Tribunal could run into several hundred pounds. The legally qualified chairman of the Tribunal and his two experienced wing members examine the transcript of the public enquiry and then usually put questions to the appellant or his advocate. Interestingly, witnesses are not required to take the oath as in normal civil or criminal court proceedings.

After careful consideration of all the evidence and relevant law the Tribunal either upholds or dismisses the appeal. Appeal from the Tribunal's finding is to the Court of Appeal.

Casenotes

1. RMC (East Midlands) Ltd v Yorkshire Traffic Area Licensing Authority 1970 1 ALL ER 890

A haulage contractor, one Gerald Robert Clewes, agreed with RMC to deliver mixed concrete to RMC's customers. Unfortunately, Mr Clewes fell sick and could not find a replacement driver. So RMC had to send one of its employees, a Mr Stacey, to drive Mr Clewes' truck. Mr Clewes held a carrier's licence (the forerunner of the O licence), required by the Road Traffic Act 1960, but RMC did not. RMC managed to fulfill its contractual commitments, with Mr Stacey driving on behalf of Mr Clewes but remaining an employee of RMC. Mr Stacey's wages, National Insurance stamp and Selective Employment Tax were all paid by RMC.

In the circumstances, the Barnsley justices found RMC guilty of using a vehicle without a carrier's licence and on appeal, the High Court confirmed this finding. RMC was the user in law and as such needed a carrier's licence.

2. Mr G's renewal application

On an application for renewal of a three-vehicle licence made by Mr G of Fawley, Hampshire, the South-eastern Licensing Authority, Mr Randall Thornton, had to consider objections from New Forest District Council and representations from local residents. The Council argued the proposed change of operating centre on tree nursery land did not conform with rural development in that area. The LA had to consider any effect which the use of an operating centre had on the local environment.

Referring to appeals before the Transport Tribunal in 1984 and early 1985, the LA had to consider the use of an operating centre as a place to keep authorized vehicles 'when not in use', an expression unfortunately not found in the Act or regulations. A more recent appeal before the Tribunal showed the movement of vehicles in the 'vicinity' could be taken into account.

Mr G gave evidence that his vehicles would not leave the operating centre before 8 am or return before 5 pm. In these circumstances, albeit with some hesitation, the LA granted a licence for two years with a condition limiting the times between which authorized vehicles could enter and leave the operating centre and a condition prohibiting the maintenance of vehicles at the operating centre.

Source: *Freight*, June 1986

3. *T W Ltd's representations*

In February 1986 the Eastern Deputy Licensing Authority (DLA) renewed T W Ltd's licence for nine vehicles and 15 trailers operating out of Thrapston, Northamptonshire, with conditions prohibiting maintenance or movement of authorized vehicles before 6 am and after 7 pm (except in an emergency) or on Sundays and public holidays.

On appeal, the Transport Tribunal directed that the matter be referred back to the DLA, Mr Humphrey Lewis, for T W Ltd to have the opportunity to make further representations concerning the constrictions placed on business operations by these conditions.

Having heard T W Ltd's further representations seeking extended hours for their haulage operations, the DLA confirmed that the conditions attaching to the licence renewal had been imposed solely to prevent local residents having their sleep disturbed at unsocial hours. This remained a most important consideration, but some relaxation of the original prohibition would not go amiss. Accordingly, the conditions were amended to allow haulage operations to start at 5 am and continue until 9 pm at the Oundle Road operating centre; Sundays and bank holidays remained inviolate.

Source: *Freight*, May 1986

4. Basildon District Council's appeal

Basildon District Council appealed to the Transport Tribunal against the grant of a licence to Rees Haulage on the basis that the proposed operating centre was unsuitable on environmental grounds. The Council explained that the operating centre had no relevant planning permission nor had any application for change of use been made to the Council. The operating centre was not suitable in planning terms and hence, the Council argued, unsuitable for a licence from the LA.

If a licence was granted the Council would have to consider issuing an enforcement notice requiring Rees Haulage to stop operations as an infringement of planning law.

The Tribunal dismissed the appeal, affirming that the LA did not exercise his statutory function to assist the local planning authority, which had different functions to perform. It was not the LA's function to do the planners' job.

Source: *Freight*, May 1986

Chapter 4
Property

An understanding of property matters is important to all hauliers. The recent liberalization of legal services which allows more people to do conveyancing may make it even more important than it has been hitherto. The aim here is not to encourage hauliers to do their own conveyancing, but to ensure they are better equipped to appreciate what the solicitor or other 'expert' is doing on their behalf.

Familiarity with two basic property documents – a lease and a conveyance – is very useful. Despite numerous campaigns to introduce ordinary language into property documents, the legal language used is still tortuous, and, as this state of affairs is unlikely to change quickly, it is worthwhile spending some time studying a typical business lease and conveyance.

The lease

The lease in our sample document can be seen to comprise five parts, as follows:

1. The premises: includes date of the lease; name, address and occupation of the landlord and the tenant; the address of the premises; and confirmation of the letting. The word *demises* is used instead of the more popular *lets*.
2. The *habendum* (meaning, in Latin, *holding*) gives the term of the lease. A lease 'from 25th December' commences at midnight 25–26th December.
3. The *reddendum* is the formal reservation of the rent by the landlord.
4. The covenants set out the formal obligations of both landlord and tenant. The tenant in breach of covenant loses the lease. The landlord in breach pays damages to the tenant.

5. The provisos and conditions for re-entry by the landlord for breach of covenant or non-payment of rent by the tenant are designed to give the landlord power to terminate the lease.

There are six essential elements of a valid lease:

1. There must be a landlord (sometimes called the lessor) with capacity to make the lease.
2. There must be a tenant (sometimes called the lessee) capable of taking the business premises demised.
3. The premises must be capable of being let.
4. The term of the lease must be clearly defined.
5. The landlord and the tenant must have a common intention to grant and take the lease.
6. Certain formalities have to be observed; for instance, the lease must be in the form of a deed if for a term of more than three years.

THIS LEASE made the day of One thousand nine hundred and eighty-seven between Albert Hardcastle of The Gamekeeper's Cottage Highfields near Scunthorpe in the County of Humberside Farmer (hereinafter called the Landlord) of the one part and Adam Swannson of 1 Delderfield Close The Kentish Hexagon near Westerham Kent Haulier (hereinafter called the Tenant) of the other part WITNESSETH as follows:

1. The landlord hereby demises unto the Tenant ALL THAT messuage or dwelling-house with the outbuildings and garden attached thereto and forming part thereof known as Number 10 Downing Lane Old Fableland in the County of Humberside which premises are outlined in red on the Plan annexed to these presents EXCEPT AND RESERVING AND SUBJECT to the exceptions and reservations set out in the Schedule hereto TO HOLD the same unto the Tenant from the 25th day of December 1986 for the term of seven years PAYING therefore the net yearly rent of £2500 clear of all deductions by equal quarterly instalments commencing on the 25th day of December 1986 next and thereafter on the usual quarter days.

2. The Tenant hereby covenants with the Landlord as follows:
   - (i) To pay the rent hereby reserved on the days and in the manner aforesaid
   - (ii) To pay all rates taxes assessments charges and outgoings which now are or may at any time hereafter be imposed assessed or charged upon the premises whether payable by the owner or occupier thereof

These covenants will usually be followed by other covenants by the Tenant including
   - (iii) *To repair and decorate internally and externally*
   - (iv) *To pay legal and other costs of proceedings and for forfeiture notices*
   - (v) *To yield up the premises in a good state of repair at the end of the lease*
   - (vi) *To alter the premises only as permitted by the Landlord*
   - (vii) *To permit the Landlord to inspect the premises*
   - (viii) *Not to assign or sub-let without the Landlord's consent (although this consent should not be withheld unreasonably)*
   - (ix) *To insure the premises.*

3. The Tenant paying the rent hereby reserved and performing and observing the covenants on the Tenant's part herein contained the Landlord hereby covenants with the Tenant as follows:
   - (i) That the Tenant may peacefully hold and enjoy the demised premises during the said term without any interruption by the Landlord or any other persons lawfully claiming through under or in trust for the Landlord.

This covenant for quiet enjoyment will be followed by other covenants by the Landlord especially the covenant to repair

4. PROVIDED ALWAYS and it is hereby expressly agreed and declared as follows:
   - (1) That if the rent hereby reserved or any part thereof shall remain unpaid for twenty-one days after the same shall have become due (whether formally demanded or not) or if any covenant on the part of the

Tenant herein contained shall not be performed or observed or if the Tenant shall become bankrupt or enter into any composition with his creditors it shall be lawful for the Landlord to re-enter upon the premises or any point thereof in the name of the whole and thereupon this demise shall absolutely determine.

(2) This demise shall not confer upon or be deemed to include (by implication or otherwise) in favour of the Tenant any right of light or air liberties privileges easements or advantages (except such as are specifically granted in this lease) in through over and upon any land or premises adjoining or near to the demised premises.

IN WITNESS etc.

(signatures seals and witnesses)

The PLAN and SCHEDULE referred to

Security of tenure

The relationship between a landlord and a tenant of business premises is governed by the general law until the landlord serves a notice to quit or the term of the lease expires. At that point special protection is given to business tenants under the Landlord and Tenant Act 1927 and Part II of the Landlord and Tenant Act 1954 as amended by Part I of the Law of Property Act 1969. Essentially, this statutory protection gives a business tenant security of tenure. A business tenant is entitled to a new contractual tenancy for a fixed term up to 14 years. If a new tenancy is not possible compensation will be available. Section 23(1) provides that Part II of the 1954 Act applies 'to any tenancy where the property comprised in the tenancy is or includes premises which are occupied by the tenant for the purposes of a business carried on by him or for those and other purposes'.

However, there are a number of technical requirements which have to be met before a tenant is granted another business tenancy or compensation. Accordingly, proper legal advice should be taken to ensure all protection available is actually taken advantage of. The case reports are littered with tales of business tenants losing their statutory rights by not complying with such technicalities as the time limit for the service of notice upon the landlord indicating an intention to renew.

Tenant's covenants

During the term of a business tenancy a haulier must comply with the tenant's covenants (promises) made to his landlord. The covenant to pay the rent on the due date, quarterly in advance usually, is absolutely fundamental. Yet it is surprising how many business tenants feel the quarter day is not very important, expecting a warning that the rent should be paid fairly soon. If rent remains outstanding for 21 days after the due date, forfeiture proceedings may be brought against a dilatory tenant by a strongwilled landlord. If these proceedings do not result in termination of the lease, a tenant will probably still have incurred considerable legal expense – payment of the landlord's legal costs for taking these forfeiture proceedings.

The covenant to repair is extremely important; interpretation can be a problem which, if not quickly settled, becomes a source of continuing hostility between landlord and tenant. And this hostility can become expensive if lawyers and surveyors have to be called in to interpret this type of covenant. It is prudent, therefore, for a tenant to try to settle any differences without going to court, even if the landlord appears pedantic and inflexible. Legal arguments about the extent and scope of repairing covenants keep much of the landlord and tenant bar in very regular work.

Covenant against assignment

One covenant which far too frequently causes legal problems concerns the reasonableness (or otherwise) of a landlord in refusing to consent to a tenant assigning his leasehold interest to another person. A landlord is bound to include a covenant against assignment and subletting if he wishes to maintain control over the business tenancy. An absolute prohibition against assignment is less popular than a qualified prohibition which requires a landlord not to withhold consent unreasonably. Not surprisingly, the shorter the lease, the more severe the prohibition becomes. The test of reasonableness of a landlord's refusal is not an entirely objective one. One writer on landlord and tenant law explains:

> If in refusing, he acted as a reasonable man would have done in the same position, because he entertained the same fears, having regard to the character of the proposed assignee, etc, the real purpose of the assignment, the effect of the assignment on the property or other property of the landlord, etc, the refusal will be upheld as reasonable.

In a number of decided cases a landlord has been held to be acting reasonably in refusing consent in these circumstances:

1. Proposed assignee objectionable for some personal or financial reason.
2. Premises might be allowed to deteriorate by the proposed assignee.
3. Landlord might be at risk financially, the subtenancy proposed being at a premium and a low rent.
4. Proposed usage would be different from that for which the premises were let.
5. Real purpose of the proposed assignment to give the assignee the right to qualify for a statutory tenancy.
6. Where there is insufficient information supplied about a proposed assignee for a proper decision to be made on the question of consent.

Certainly very careful enquiries will normally be made by a landlord before seriously entertaining an assignment or subtenancy. A haulier wishing to divest himself of an unwanted business tenancy should appreciate, therefore, that this course of action may prove quite difficult.

Covenant to insure

Apart from short leases, it has long been the practice for business tenancies to provide expressly for insurance of premises against fire and other damage. It is commonplace for the landlord to effect insurance for business premises and to seek reimbursement of the premium from the tenant.

The insurance is normally placed with a well known national insurance company or a company approved by the landlord. In practice the tenant has little influence on the choice of insurer. If business premises suffer serious fire damage the landlord usually covenants to reinstate the premises with all convenient speed. The tenant need not pay rent until the business premises are put back in working order again.

Purchase of business premises

The alternative to leasing is, of course, to buy premises – if you can afford to do so. The haulage contractor wishing to buy premises will naturally instruct a solicitor (or other expert) to handle the purchase. But an awareness of what is involved in the purchase deed (called a conveyance where land is unregistered, and a 'transfer' if it is registered) can be very helpful.

To take an example: Adam Swannson wishes to purchase a garage in Gloucestershire, to use as a workshop for his vehicles. Swannson already has a depot in Swindon but it is a condition of his O licence for that operating centre that maintenance can only be carried out in a restricted manner. So Swannson-on-Wheels will gain considerable benefit from the purchase of a relatively local garage facility on the outskirts of Tetbury.

The purchase price has been agreed at £5000, and the form of the conveyance follows a conventional pattern.

THIS CONVEYANCE is made the   day of July One thousand nine hundred and eighty-seven BETWEEN ALAN BROWN of Lime Cottage Tetbury in the County of Gloucester Fireman (hereinafter called "the Vendor") of the one part and ADAM SWANNSON of 1 Delderfield Close the Kentish Hexagon near Westerham in the County of Kent (hereinafter called "the Purchaser") of the other part

WHEREAS

1. THE Vendor was granted the fee simple of the property hereinafter described by a Conveyance dated the 9th day of July One thousand nine hundred and fifty-one made between Lloyds Bank Limited of 71 Lombard Street in the

City of London and the Vendor the legal estate to the said property having vested in the said Vendor by such grant.

2. THE Vendor is seized of the property hereinafter described for an estate in fee simple in possession free from encumbrances save as hereinafter mentioned and has agreed with the Purchaser for the sale to him of the said property for a like estate at the price of five thousand pounds

NOW THIS DEED WITNESSETH

1. IN pursuance of the said agreement and in consideration of the sum of FIVE THOUSAND POUNDS now paid by the Purchaser to the Vendor (the receipt of which sum the Vendor hereby acknowledges) the Vendor as beneficial owner hereby conveys unto the Purchaser ALL THAT Garage known as Number 47 West Street aforesaid in the County of Gloucester all which said property is more particularly described in the annexed plan and outlined in red TO HOLD the same unto the Purchaser in fee simple together with the benefit of but subject also to a restrictive covenant contained in a Conveyance dated the Twenty-fifth day of May One thousand nine hundred and thirty-four made between the Stroud Brewery Company Limited of the one part and William Thomson deceased of the other part but otherwise free from incumbrances.

2. WITH the object and intent of affording to the Vendor a full and sufficient indemnity but not further or otherwise the Purchaser hereby covenants with the Vendor that he the Purchaser and the persons deriving title under him will at all times hereafter duly observe and perform the covenants contained or referred to in the Conveyance so far as the same affect the property hereby conveyed and remain to be observed and performed and are capable of being enforced and will indemnify and keep indemnified the Vendor and his successors in title from and against all actions costs claims and demands in respect of any breach non-observance or non-performance thereof so far as aforesaid

3. IT IS HEREBY CERTIFIED that the transaction hereby effected does not form part of a larger transaction or of a series of transactions in respect of which the amount of

value or the aggregate amount of value of the consideration exceeds thirty thousand pounds.
SIGNED SEALED AND DELIVERED etc.

Chapter 5

Tax and How to Minimize it

Small haulage businesses trading as limited companies are typical of the road transport industry, so the incidence of tax on these firms is worth some examination.

Small companies rate taxation

The small companies rate is applied to companies with fairly small taxable profits – below £100,000 in 1987. While the full corporation tax rate between 1 April 1986 and 31 March 1987 stood at 35 per cent, the small companies rate was 29 per cent. Following the 1987 budget this rate will be 27 per cent for the tax year 1987–88.

Capital gains tax (CGT)

CGT for an individual is calculated on the basis that the first £6300 net gains are exempt, and gains over £6300 attract a tax rate of 30 per cent. This exemption is not available to companies.

In the first three years of trading, the haulier should be careful not to make any chargeable gains for tax purposes. Liability to capital gains tax arises where a chargeable gain is made on the disposal of company assets. The term 'disposal' means a change in ownership. The term 'assets' refers to virtually all forms of property, including stocks and shares, land and buildings. Given the wide scope of the charge to CGT, a large number of exemptions from this tax bite are granted to make the system fair and workable. A company may be able to avoid CGT liability even though it has made gains of a capital nature, by means of various reliefs and allowances.

Retirement relief

The director of a haulage company who would like to retire as soon as is practicable and leave much of the management of the firm to his children may take advantage of retirement relief. This type of relief is of great benefit to the retiring director upon the disposal of his shares in the company, providing he has kept a sufficient percentage holding of shares and has been a full-time working director until this point in time. Retirement relief could not be claimed on disposals before 6 April 1985 unless the individual concerned had reached the age of 60. The relief available then increased progressively from age 60, reaching the maximum of £100,000 at age 65. (The minimum age is still 60). New rules make it possible to obtain the maximum relief from CGT at age 60. The 1987 budget raised the sum available to £125,000.

It should be noted that for a person obliged to retire from business because of failing health, the maximum relief can be obtained before the age of 60 (given a ten year period as director). An individual must have been in the business for ten years or have retained shares throughout this period to qualify for maximum relief. The first part of the relief becomes available one full year after disposal of the shares, and the rest is available in equal instalments over the following nine years.

Roll-over relief

The directors of a haulage company will be keen to avoid CGT when replacing equipment which, through market forces, has actually increased in value, with new equipment which is more suitable for the firm's purposes. A gain in the value of a piece of equipment used for business purposes may be 'rolled over' and offset against the cost of obtaining the replacement equipment. The cost of the replacement equipment is thus reduced and may attract CGT when it is disposed of; but for the time being, liability for CGT is avoided.

This type of relief extends to land and buildings used for business purposes. A goodwill payment also benefits from roll-over relief.

Indexation allowance

With inflation at even a relatively modest rate, the value of business assets can increase, creating a liability for CGT upon disposal.

For an asset disposed of after 5 April 1985, a form of relief known as an indexation allowance may be claimed. This allowance is calculated by reference to the RI and the RD factors. RI stands for the figure shown in the retail price index for March 1982 or the month in which expenditure was incurred, whichever is the later. RD stands for the index figure for the month in which the disposal occurs.

The allowance is the product of:

$$\frac{RD - RI}{RI} \times \text{expenditure}$$

An indexation allowance can also be used to inflate or create a loss for CGT purposes.

CGT calculation

Allowable losses for CGT purposes from a previous year of tax assessment may be brought forward to diminish the value of gains for calculation of CGT in the current year of assessment. For small companies, only a fraction of the capital gains are charged; in the year ending 31 March 1987 this is six-sevenths.

Tax deductions

Generally speaking, the calculation of chargeable gains and allowable losses for companies is the same as that used for individuals paying personal tax. The haulier's tax bill can be minimized by taking full advantage of the various losses and deductions allowable against income.

The latest edition of *Year-end Tax Planning for Companies* is very useful in monitoring a company's financial progress. It includes the following checklist for tax deductions and tax losses:

- Have you considered accelerating capital expenditure plans on plant and industrial buildings?
- Have you considered hire purchase and leasing as well as outright purchase?
- Have you considered expansion in an enterprise zone?
- Have you considered the payment of interest before the year end?
- Have bonuses to directors and staff been considered?
- Have you considered a profit sharing scheme?
- Have tax losses been utilized?

Share option schemes

The principal advantage of a share option scheme, approved by the Revenue under the Finance Act 1984, is that key personnel can be rewarded with an equity holding in return for continuing loyalty and enterprise.

Share options are more attractive than outright share purchases because there is no risk of a loss being made by the employee taking up the option if share prices fall. Furthermore, the actual price of the shares only has to be paid upon exercising the share option. The actual exercise of this option may not be made earlier than three years nor later than ten years after it has been obtained.

VAT

A haulier must register for VAT if there are reasonable grounds for believing that its contracts will bring in more than a certain sum per year. This sum was raised from £20,500 to £21,300 in the 1987 budget.

Payment of VAT has to be made at the end of each quarter; that is 31 March, 30 June, 30 September and 31 December. At the time of writing, payment is required by HM Customs & Excise from all registered companies on sales invoiced, not on income actually received. However, the 1987 budget proposals are for firms with an annual turnover under £250,000 to be able to pay VAT on a cash basis viz. VAT need only be paid when the invoice bearing VAT has actually been paid. Such small firms will be required to account for VAT once a year, and then only on bills actually paid. This will considerably help cash flow problems for new haulage firms and hauliers still operating at a modest turnover.

Inheritance tax

This is a tax which affects the disposition of assets on death.

Unitl 12 March 1975, liability to estate duty was governed by complicated provisions contained in the Finance Act 1894, as amended. After this date, and until 18 March 1986, a form of death duty called capital transfer tax applied. The current form of death duty is called inheritance tax. This new tax still imposes a liability on the value of an individual's estate at death, but does not apply to gifts made *inter vivos* (also called lifetime gifts).

Inheritance tax applies to the total value of the deceased's assets, so the directors of a haulage company need to be aware of the tax bite on their highly prized commercial wealth. Let us see how the tax operates by taking the example of a haulage firm whose managing director died on 31 December 1986.

The issued share capital of the company, consisting of 100 ordinary shares of £1 each, was divided 50:30:20 among its three directors. On 31 December 1986 the managing director still held 50 ordinary shares in the company. An independent share valuation would have given these shares a total value of about £50,000. As the managing director had held this controlling shareholding interest for at least two years, it attracted business assets relief of 50 per cent. The value of shares of £50,000 less 50 per cent left £25,000 as the value to be included in the estate for inheritance tax purposes.

Had it been the director with a retained shareholding of 30 shares who had died on 31 December 1986, his estate too would have had the benefit of business assets relief, but at a lower percentage deduction. As a minority shareholding interest in an unquoted company, his shares would have attracted only 30 per cent relief, leaving £21,000 (£30,000 – £9,000) for inclusion in his estate for inheritance tax purposes.

In 1986 tax liability was abolished on gifts made outright to individuals or put into trusts for children, as long as the donor survives seven years from the date of the gift. As with the old estate duty system, there is a form of 'taper' relief which reduces the tax payable on the gift if death occurs more than three, but less than seven years after making the gift.

But this relief benefits only the really wealthy who can afford to give away substantial chunks of capital. If the gift falls within the donor's nil rate band – currently £71,000 (but increased to £90,000 under the budget) – no tax would be payable, and as no tax is paid, there is nothing to claim taper relief against. But the full value of the gift – and this is the tax trap – continues to be added to determine the rate of tax payable on his remaining estate.

It is clear that the directors of a haulage company who are not in the 'really wealthy' category need very sound tax planning advice on the likely impact of the inheritance tax legislation. (The really wealthy need very special advice!)

Tax changes

Tax planning needs to be constantly under review. Every year we have a new finance bill which sets lawyers and accountants considerable problems of interpretation. At least once a year, and preferably every six months, the haulier should take advice from his accountant on ways in which to minimize his tax burden.

Before taking professional advice, the haulier should familiarize himself with basic facts about taxation, especially recent changes in the law. The budget of 17 March 1987 included the following changes:

Income tax: Basic rate reduced from 29p to 27p in the £. Single person's allowance up £90 to £2425; married man's allowance up to £3795. Higher rate taxation at 40 per cent starts at £17,900 per annum.

Payment-by-results: Companies are to be encouraged to pay employees according to profits made. Fifty per cent of all profit-related pay up to £3000 per annum or 20 per cent of total pay will be tax-free.

Pensions: Tax relief will be available for people making their own pension arrangements independently of employers or the state.

VAT: See section on VAT above.

Inheritance tax: A threshold change – up from £71,000 to £90,000.

Cars: Car benefits enjoyed by company employees are to be taxed by a further 10 per cent.

Business taxation: Small companies tax rate reduced from 29 per cent to 27 per cent; so, too, advance corporation tax. Corporation tax on capital gains made by companies will be charged as income at the normal corporation tax rate (35 per cent or 29 per cent).

Capital gains tax: Retirement relief limit increased from £100,000 to £125,000. Annual exempt amount increased from £6300 to £6600, taking into account the effect of inflation.

Training: Tax relief will be given to employers helping employees leaving their company to set up on their own.

Chapter 6
Taking Out Insurance

Taking out proper insurance to cover the risks entailed in operating a haulage business is not as easy as it might appear. The wording of insurance policies is often complicated. The exemption clauses in particular, by which the insurer seeks to limit his liability to the haulier, can be very extensive. Careful reading of the various clauses in a policy often reveals that surprisingly little is actually insured against. It is the broker's job to make sure the haulier fully understands the small print of the exemption and other clauses. The broker may need to be made aware of this duty. The mistake is often made of leaving too much to the insurance broker – not giving him sufficiently clear instructions and then, most importantly, not checking with him that the policy taken out does cover the risks which need to be insured against. The haulier should therefore take the utmost care in selecting a good insurance broker and then take advantage of his skill and expertise. Simply paying the insurance premium each year without enquiring what cover is currently advantageous does not amount to good business. One quick way of going out of business is to be unable to meet a substantial claim because it is not covered by insurance. Even a claim which is litigated and defended successfully in court usually involves unimaginable loss of time, aggravation and payment of high legal costs (which are rarely recovered in full from the unsuccessful claimant). If a claim is lost in court, the pain, loss and damage suffered by the haulier is obviously much greater. It is essential to have good professional advice, and to review the adequacy of your insurance cover from time to time.

Vehicle insurance

The requirement that all motor vehicles (except invalid carriages, police and local authority vehicles) used on a road must be covered by third party insurance is fundamental to the lawful operation of any haulage business. (The insurance company is the first party, the insured the second and anyone else the third party.)

Insurance cover must be taken out with an insurance company which is a member of the Motor Insurers' Bureau (MIB). When anyone dies or suffers physical injury at the hands of a motorist who is not covered by third party insurance, the MIB steps in and compensates the victim. This is a very valuable function, considering the number of uninsured motorists on our roads.

Certificate of insurance

Insurance cover comes into force only when a certificate of insurance, confirming the terms of the cover, is actually received.

A typical certificate of motor insurance for a haulier is shown below. For administrative reasons, a simple code (five letters in our example) is used to state who may drive the vehicle, the limitations as to use and the exclusions from cover. A clerical error remaining unnoticed and uncorrected can have disastrous consequences, so it is essential to make sure the certificate does properly reflect the insurance required.

Clause B of the certificate entitles 'any person driving on the order or with the permission of the Policyholder' to drive. In a haulage firm it is prudent to make sure that everyone knows who does in fact have permission to drive; this avoids the problems which arise if a vehicle driven by someone in the firm without authority is involved in an accident. No haulier can afford to be complacent on this issue.

Clause L of the certificate restricts the policyholder to the towing of just one trailer. If a haulier wished to tow other items under the terms of this policy, an additional clause is needed to clarify the extent of cover; otherwise the insurers might not accept liability.

Clause T excludes cover for the carriage of passengers for hire or reward. Sometimes the line between co-driver and paying passenger can be very thin. Accordingly, drivers should be warned of the consequences of infringing this particular clause.

CERTIFICATE OF MOTOR INSURANCE

1. **Description of Vehicles.**
   Any motor vehicle owned by the Policyholder or
   hired to him under a hire-purchase agreement.

Certificate No. **M.V.**

016/ 1548299/27/03

2. **Name of Policyholder.**

**BARRY L BROWN & JOHN CHARLES BROWN T/A
BROWNS TRANSPORT EUROPE**

3. **Effective date of the
   Commencement of Insurance for** 28 MAR 1986
   the purposes of the relevant Law.

4. **Date of Expiry of Insurance.**

   27 MAR 1987

5. **Persons or Classes of Persons entitled to drive.**

   Those specified by Clause(s) **A B** providing that the person driving holds a licence to drive the
   vehicle or has held and is not disqualified for holding or obtaining such a licence.
   A. The Policyholder.
   B. Any person driving on the order or with the permission of the Policyholder.
   C. Any person in the Policyholder's employment under a contract of service driving on the order or with
   the permission of the Policyholder.
   D. Any hirer of the vehicle or any person driving on the order or with the permission of such hirer.
   E. Any person to whom the vehicle is let on hire by the Policyholder.
   F.

6. **Limitations as to use.**
   As defined by Clause(s) **G L** subject to **Exclusion(s) T** and the additional exclusion of
   racing pacemaking reliability trial or speedtesting.
   G. Policyholder's business or social domestic and pleasure; including the carriage of passengers.
   H. Policyholder's business.
   K. Agricultural forestry and on behalf of Public Authorities for snow frost and ice clearance; including
   the carriage of passengers.
   L. Towing not more than one trailer or (other than for reward) one disabled mechanically-propelled
   vehicle.
   M. Social domestic and pleasure by the Policyholder.
   N. Carriage of passengers.
   O. Carriage of passengers or goods in connection with the Policyholder's business excluding commercial
   travelling other than by the person to whom the vehicle has been hired by the Policyholder.
   P. Social domestic pleasure and business by any person to whom the vehicle is let on hire by the
   Policyholder.
   Q. Business of the Policyholder or of any hirer of the Vehicle.
   R. Stage Express or Contract Carriage.

   Exclusions.
   S. Hire or reward.
   T. Carriage of passengers for hire or reward.
   U. Hire or reward other than the carriage of passengers.
   V. Commercial travelling or any purpose in connection with the Motor Trade.
   W. Hire or reward other than the carriage of passengers for Private Hire which term shall mean the
   letting of the vehicle supplied to the hirer direct from the Policyholder's garage.
   X. Standing or plying for hire in any street, road or public place.
   Y. Towing a greater number of trailers in all than is permitted by law.
   Z. Towing a trailer except the towing (other than for reward) of any one disabled mechanically propelled
   vehicle.
   ZA.Towing a trailer except (i) a trailer partially superimposed upon the power unit or (ii) the power unit
   towing (other than for reward) any one disabled mechanically-propelled vehicle.

I hereby certify that the Policy to which this Certificate relates satisfies the requirements of the relevant Law
applicable in Great Britain, Northern Ireland, the Isle of Man, the Island of Guernsey, the Island of Jersey and the
Island of Alderney.
General Accident Fire and Life Assurance Corporation p.l.c.
AUTHORISED INSURERS

HEAD OFFICE:
PITHEAVLIS, PERTH, SCOTLAND PH2 0NH

Chief General Manager

NOTE: For full details of the insurance cover reference should be made to the policy.

D.P. 44 M **WARNING** *For change of vehicle, transfer of interest, suspension
or termination of insurance - SEE OVER* ✱ 2 ✱

Exemption clauses

A clause which purports to exclude liability in a contract may be unreasonable in the light of the Unfair Contract Terms Act 1977. The haulier should be aware of this possibility, especially in the context of insurance cover, where the obligation on him is to act in the utmost good faith when disclosing material facts on the proposal form. Under the 1977 Act, Section 2:

1. A person cannot by reference to any contract terms or to a notice given to persons generally or to particular persons exclude or restrict his liability for death or personal injury resulting from negligence.
2. In the case of other loss or damage, a person cannot so exclude or restrict his liability for negligence except in so far as the term or notice satisfies the requirement of reasonableness.
3. Where a contract term or notice purports to exclude or restrict liability for negligence a person's agreement to or awareness of it is not of itself to be taken as indicating his voluntary acceptance of any risk.

Under the 1977 Act, in order to decide whether a term or notice is reasonable, particular attention is paid to:

(a) the resources which he could expect to be available to him for the purpose of meeting the liability should it arise; and
(b) how far it was open to him to cover himself by insurance.

Green Card system

The MIB concept extends internationally by means of the Green Card system. The Green Card is issued at the start of the international journey. Most European countries have bureaux equivalent to the MIB. The names and addresses of these bureaux are listed in Appendix I. A Green Card furnished at frontiers ensures smooth passage establishing as it does the existence of a country's compulsory motor insurance. In theory, EEC countries do not need production of a Green Card, but in practice most hauliers carry one to facilitate an uninterrupted crossing. Despite an EEC directive requiring member states to have motor policies giving automatic compulsory cover, not all countries in the Green Card system are within the terms of the directive.

Goods in transit (GIT)

The haulier must insure the goods he carries against loss or damage. This is a standard condition of the Road Haulage Association insurance cover. Unfortunately, a maximum liability of £800 per ton is usually applied for goods in transit in the UK. Low value consignments are easily covered by this facility, but for the haulier carrying a more valuable load, such as video equipment or other luxury consumer durables, additional cover has to be taken. If high value loads are carried regularly, an appropriate annual premium should be sought. The occasional carriage of higher risk loads should only attract once-off premiums. The following definition of the GIT cover secured by a GIT hauliers policy with the Commercial Union Assurance Company is typical:

(a) While being loaded upon carried by or unloaded from any of the Insured's vehicles specified in the Schedule or any vehicle used to complete the journey in the event of the said vehicle breaking down en route.

(b) While temporarily unloaded from any of the said vehicles in the course of a journey for a period of up to 72 hours (not counting Sunday or any Public Holiday) anywhere in England Scotland or Wales.

A haulier can make it a condition that he incurs no liability under these circumstances:

- act of God
- act of war or civil war
- seizure under legal process
- act or omission of the trader, his employees or agents
- inherent liability to wastage in bulk, or weight, latent defect or inherent defect vice or natural deterioration of the merchandise
- insufficient or improper packing
- insufficient labelling or addressing
- riots, civil commotions, strikes, lock-outs, stoppage or

restraint of labour from whatever cause
- consignee not taking or accepting delivery within a reasonable time
- loss of a particular market whether held daily or at intervals
- indirect or consequential damages
- fraud on the part of the trader (in this context trader means either consignor or consignee)
- if non-delivery of a consignment, whether in part or whole, is not notified in writing within a specified number of days of despatch and a claim made in writing within a further specified number of days of despatch
- if pilferage or damage is not notified in writing within a specified number of days of delivery, and a claim made in writing within a further specified number of days of delivery.

It is essential that customers are aware of any conditions of carriage. All business stationery – invoices, letters, quotations, delivery notes and so on – must therefore refer to these conditions. A standard term of GIT insurance requires a haulier to confirm to his insurance company that he has notified all his customers of the conditions of carriage.

The RHA's own conditions of carriage, together with a set of explanatory notes, can be found in *The Transport Manager's Handbook*. Only RHA members are entitled to use these conditions.

For further illustration, let us take the case of Browns Transport Europe (BTE).

BTE, with two vehicles and main depot near Bromley are considering a new additional depot at the Dartford International Ferry Terminal on Stone Marshes, Dartford (DIFT) near the Dartford Tunnel on the south bank of the River Thames. One of the vehicles based near Bromley may now operate from DIFT and loads would no longer be European general haulage, rather international consignments of pharmaceutical products and electronic goods passing through DIFT.

The type of GIT insurance suitable for BTE (as an associate member of the FTA) in these circumstances would be in the form of the specimen policy below. There are insurance brokers offering policy terms who are used by the members of the Freight Transport Association upon express recommendation of that body.

Road Hauliers
Goods in Transit Policy
Please read this Policy carefully and
see that it meets your requirements

The National Transit
INSURANCE COMPANY LIMITED

A member of
Sun Alliance Insurance Group

Head Office: Voysey House Barley Mow Passage
Chiswick London W4 4PZ Telephone: 01-995 1551

This Policy and the Schedule shall be read together and any word or expression to which a specific meaning has been attached in either shall bear such meaning wherever it may appear

Whereas the Insured by the Proposal which shall be the basis of and incorporated in this Contract have applied to the Company for the insurance contained herein and have agreed to pay the Premium set out in the Schedule hereto

Indemnity
The Company will subject to the terms limits conditions and exceptions contained herein and/or endorsed hereon indemnify the Insured if during the Period of Insurance any of the Property shall be lost destroyed or damaged whilst being carried by loaded upon or off-loaded from the Vehicles (including while temporarily stored in the course of transit whether loaded upon or off-loaded from the Vehicles) to the extent to which there is a liability upon the Insured for such loss destruction or damage under
a) the Road Haulage Association Limited Conditions of Carriage (as specified in the Proposal form) or
b) the Insureds Own Conditions of Carriage (as attached to this Policy) or
c) the Convention on the Contract for the International Carriage of Goods by Road hereinafter referred to as CMR or
d) Common Law where the Conditions of Carriage in a) and b) above cannot be applied and where CMR does not apply
In addition the Company will indemnify the Insured for
   i) their liability for transhipment recovery and debris removal charges following loss destruction of or damage to the Property or an accident to the vehicle conveying such Property
   ii) transhipment or recovery charges incurred by the Insured to mitigate or prevent any claim
   iii) loss destruction of or damage to sheets ropes pallets dunnage chains toggles and the like but not for wear and tear

Exceptions – the Company shall not indemnify the Insured for
1 Loss destruction of or damage to documents cash (including bank and currency notes) or bullion
2 Loss destruction death of or injury to any living creature
3 Household office or factory removals
4 Loss of market loss of profits or any consequential loss of any nature whatsoever
5 Deterioration and/or depreciation unless caused by fire theft or as a direct result of collision of the conveying vehicle or overturning of the conveying vehicle
6 Delay (including claims under article 23(5) of CMR) unless loss destruction of or damage to the Property has resulted from such delay when the Company will indemnify the Insured against their liability for such delay in a sum not exceeding the Carriage Charge
7 Storage of property at a rental or under a contract for storage and distribution

8 a) loss or destruction of or damage to any property whatsoever or any expense whatsoever resulting or arising therefrom or any consequential loss
   b) any legal liability of whatsoever nature
directly or indirectly caused by or contributed to by
   i) ionising radiations or contamination by radioactivity from any nuclear fuel or from any nuclear waste from the combustion of nuclear fuel
   ii) the radioactive toxic explosive or other hazardous properties of any explosive nuclear assembly or nuclear component thereof
9 Loss destruction or damage caused by or arising from
   a) war invasion act of foreign enemy hostilities (whether war be declared or not) military or usurped power strikes riots civil commotion revolution rebellion insurrection civil war
   b) confiscation or requisition or destruction or damage by order of any Government or other Officials or Authorities

021047-1 (6-83)

Interpretation

For the purposes of this Policy Proposal shall mean any signed proposal form and declaration and any information in connection with this insurance supplied by or on behalf of the Insured in addition thereto or in substitution therefor

General Conditions

1 The Insured shall not by agreement accept liability in excess of the Road Haulage Association Limited Conditions of Carriage (as specified in the Proposal form) or the Insureds Own Conditions of Carriage (as attached to this Policy) as the case may be nor accept any special declaration of value under Articles 24 and 26 of CMR without the prior agreement of the Company

2 On the happening of any event giving rise or which might give rise to a claim under this Policy the Insured shall (at their own expense) immediately upon its coming to their knowledge
a) give written notice to the Company or the Branch referred to in the Schedule
b) submit within 7 working days (or such further time as the Company may permit) a detailed claim in writing and supply such further particulars as may be reasonably required
c) give immediate notice to the police if theft is suspected

3 This Policy shall be voidable in the event of misrepresentation misdescription or non disclosure in any material particular

4 If any claim be in any respect fraudulent or if any fraudulent means or devices be used by the Insured or anyone acting on their behalf to obtain any benefit under this Policy or if any loss destruction or damage be occasioned by the wilful act or with the connivance of the Insured or by any relative of the Insured all benefit under this Policy shall be forfeited

5 This Policy does not indemnify the Insured in respect of any claim made against them for which the Insured are or would but for the existence of this Policy be entitled to indemnity under any other policy except in respect of any excess beyond the amount payable by such other policy

6 The Insured under this Policy shall at the request and at the expense of the Company do and concur in doing and permit to be done all such acts and things as may be necessary or reasonably required by the Company for the purpose of defending any claim against the Insured enforcing any rights and remedies or of obtaining relief or indemnity from other parties to which the Company shall be or would become entitled or subrogated upon its paying for or making good any loss destruction or damage under this Policy whether such acts and things shall be or become necessary or required before or after their indemnification by the Company

7 The Company shall be entitled to take over and conduct in the name of the Insured the defence or settlement of any claim or to institute or prosecute in the name of the Insured for their own benefit any claim for indemnity or damages or otherwise and shall have full discretion in the conduct of any proceedings or in the settlement of any claim and the Insured shall give all such information and assistance as the Company may require

8 The Policy may be terminated at any time at the option of the Company provided that 30 days notice to that effect be given in writing by pre-paid letter post to the last known address of the Insured or their Broker or Agent in which case the Company shall be liable to repay on demand a ratable proportion of the Premium for the unexpired term from the date of termination

9 The benefit of this Policy shall in no circumstances whatsoever pass to any subcontractor or the Insurers of any subcontractor

10 Payment of the Premium and the due observance and fulfillment of the terms and Conditions so far as they relate to anything to be done or complied with by the Insured and the truth of the statements and answers in the Proposal shall be Conditions precedent to any liability of the Company to make any payment under this Policy

11 The Insured shall not at any one time own or operate more Vehicles or Trailers than the number specified in the Schedule

Schedule

SEC

Policy No. LN 4526

Company	The National Transit Insurance Company Limited (Incorporated in England)
Branch	West End
Agency	17D 2710 Campbell Irvine Limited
Insured	Browns Transport Europe (J C Brown and B L Brown t/as) 30A Arthur Road Biggin Hill Westerham Kent TN16 3DD

Period of Insurance	First Premium	Renewal Premium
a), From 19th August 1983		
To 4 pm on 19th August 1984 (Renewal Date)	£150.00	£150.00
b) Any subsequent period for which the Insured shall pay and the Company shall agree to accept the Renewal Premium		

The Property
a) Goods and/or Merchandise for which the Insured are responsible but excluding Goods and/or Merchandise owned by hired by or leased or loaned to the Insured
b) Containers and/or Flats for which the Insured are responsible but excluding such Containers and/or Flats owned by hired by or leased or loaned to the Insured
Trailers of any description are excluded

Particulars of the Vehicles
a) Vehicles/Trailers owned/operated by the Insured — included/~~not included~~
b) Vehicles/Trailers of Sub-contractors — ~~included~~/not included
c) Maximum number of Vehicles/Trailers owned/operated by the Insured referred to in Condition 11 is 1 (ONE)

Total Sum Insured (which is the maximum sum payable for any claim or series of claims arising out of any one happening or event) — £ 14,000.00
The maximum liability of the Company in respect of any one load is — £ 14,000.00

Excess
a) The Insured shall bear the first £25 of each and every claim other than for Containers/Flats

b) The Insured shall bear the first £100 of each and every claim for Containers/Flats

Territorial Limits
Anywhere within the United Kingdom (defined as England Scotland Wales Northern Ireland Channel Islands Isle of Man and the off-shore islands) and the Republic of Ireland

and the Continent of Europe

including sea transits within these limits

Signed on the 18th October 1983

Examined

Subject also to the following:-

VSR12

Excluding Theft from vehicle(s) left unattended in Italy

No liability shall be accepted by the Company in respect of claims for theft of or from a vehicle left unattended whilst in Italy

031073 (10-81)

VSR12

Zeebrugge ferry disaster

While this book has concentrated on domestic rules applying to haulage operations, the sinking of the Herald of Free Enterprise off Zeebrugge harbour on the night of 6th March, 1987, reminds the haulier that international rules and regulations covering compensation claims can seem very legalistic and not entirely reasonable. Limitations on the amount recoverable for loss of life (some £38,000 under the 1974 Athens Convention) and for losses to cargo and vehicles show that the haulier has to be very careful when undertaking operations involving cross-channel ferries. It must now be a matter of top priority for hauliers to take the best insurance advice available on the risks being run and the cover available for operations by road and sea to mainland Europe. Before the Zeebrugge disaster many hauliers were frankly complacent about these matters. Unfortunately, it has taken a major tragedy to focus the minds of hauliers and their professional advisers sharply on these problem areas. In an attempt to learn as much as possible from the capsize of the Herald of Free Enterprise the Treasury Solicitor has asked questions which should help to prevent a similar disaster ever recurring. These questions will be answered by the ferry inquiry to be held in London.

Heads of claim

Following the Zeebrugge ferry disaster, the haulier should be aware of some of the heads of claim which might arise when such a terrible incident occurs. For the survivor who suffered relatively minor physical injuries but was subjected to a horrific experience, compensation will be sought for psychological trauma/nervous shock. This head of claim has been called the 'walk away' category. It is a most important head of damages. Lawyers specialising in disaster claims (for example the well known firm of Pannone Napier solicitors) have to consider the medico-legal aspects of such claims carefully.

Damages in fatal accident cases are likely to be substantial and should not be underestimated. Where there is a loss of a wife/mother who did not receive income from the deceased there is still a claim for loss of housekeeping services. The extent of such a claim can be seen in the cases of Hay v Hughes 1975 1 AER 257, Regan v Williamson 1976 2 AER 241 and Mehmet v Perry 1972 2 AER 529.

In the case of a claim for bereavement in the Zeebrugge ferry disaster, Pannone and Napier explain that anomalous situations arise from the Administration of Justice Act 1982, for example:

(i) the absence of any bereavement payment of £3,500 to persons other than a spouse or parent who has lost a child under 18. In a case where parents and/or close next of kin have lost a child or close relative aged over 18 but without dependants the claim is limited to funeral expenses and property/luggage only.

(ii) the fact that the bereavement sum of £3,500 is arbitrary and was set five years ago.

The solicitors for P & O, the owners of the Townsend Thoresen ferry Herald of Free Enterprise, naturally face claims for loss of or damage to vehicles. It is understood that these solicitors (Norton Rose) have asked claimants to look to their own insurers first and that any claims in addition will be met up to the £2,700 Convention limit.

Claims for loss of cargo should present some nice legal arguments. The Steering Committee acting for many claimants has advised that all claims concerning cargo should be made to:

Charles Taylor & Co,
International House,
1 St Catherine's Way,
London E1 9UN
Tel: 01–488 3494 (contact Mr Charles Mawdsley).

Claims brought in respect of loss of cargo will be governed by the rules laid down in the Carriage of Goods by Sea Act 1971, the Hague-Visby Rules. Under these rules the carrier is entitled to limit its liability to the sum of £530 'per package or unit'. By virtue of Article iv Rule 5(E) of the Hague-Visby Rules: 'Neither the carrier nor the ship shall be entitled to the benefit of the limitation of liability provided for in this paragraph if it is proved that the damage resulted from an act or omission of the carrier done with intent to cause damage or recklessly and with knowledge that damage would probably result.' This is a most important limitation. It is understood that while the insurers of Townsend Car Ferries Limited have admitted liability in negligence no concession has been made as to recklessness. No doubt there will be some complicated arguments about the concept of recklessness in the civil courts since this concept, commonplace in the criminal courts, is rarely paraded in front of the civil judge.

The argument that, quite apart from the question of recklessness, the Convention on Limitation of Liability for Maritime Claims 1976 (which only came into force in the UK in December 1986) does as a matter of law override the limitation provisions of both the Hague-Visby Rules and the Athens Convention (for passenger claims) will not be easily accepted by Norton Rose.

In addition to compensation received under an out of court settlement, as a result of litigation or from insurers, in the case of such terrible incidents as the Zeebrugge ferry disaster, there will usually be special funds set up to assist the suffering. In April 1987 the Channel Ferry Disaster Fund had received some £3.45 million of which about £300,000 had been paid out by Trustees in the form of interim payments. The Townsend Thoresen Disaster Fund, the Townsend Thoresen Crew Fund and the P & O Additional Fund have all been established to provide extra money for those who have lost relatives as a result of the Zeebrugge disaster.

In summary, the Zeebrugge tragedy has reminded the haulier that operations across the Channel can pose quite complicated legal problems concerning matters of compensation for loss of life, injury and damage to property. It is essential, when embarking upon such operations, to have a clear understanding of the rules which will apply if disaster strikes.

Chapter 7
Employment Law

There has been an enormous amount of employment legislation in the last decade or so, and haulage companies have had to integrate this with the already extensive legal requirements which govern their operations. This has not been at all easy. The fact that drivers – unlike, say, factory workers – have to work independently to some extent, so that their schedules cannot be fixed in advance, is one reason why employment law is particularly hard to grapple with in the haulage industry. The other serious difficulty which employers in other industries do not have to cope with is that of obtaining factual details about incidents which have taken place many miles from home. This chapter aims to clarify the important issues. (For a more detailed review of employment law and practice than is possible here, the haulier is recommended to refer to *The Penguin Guide to the Law* by John Pritchard.)

The employment contract made between employer and employee still forms the basis of modern employment law, notwithstanding the detailed legislation of recent years. It need not be in writing, but a written contract is preferable as it reduces the possible grounds for misunderstanding. Even if the contract is not in writing, the haulier must serve a written statement on every employee within 13 weeks of the start of employment, outlining the basic terms of his or her employment. In the absence of a full contract of employment, these so-called 'written particulars' are usually the best evidence of the terms agreed between employer and employee.

Written particulars

The written particulars which must be provided in compliance with Section 1 Employment Protection (Consolidation) Act 1978 cover the names of employer and employee, the date employment began, pay, job title, holidays, pension rights, the employer's rules about sickness and injury, termination of employment (notice), hours of work, disciplinary and grievance procedures.

If an employee does not receive the written particulars he is entitled to, he can theoretically apply to the industrial tribunal for an order declaring what these particulars should say.

An example of written particulars is given below.

STATEMENT UNDER
EMPLOYMENT PROTECTION ACT 1978

The Humberside Heavy Haulage Company Ltd (the company)
Name of driver: Alan Wilson
Start of employment: 6 October 1986
Particulars given: 13 October 1986

1. You are employed as a class HGV1 driver with this company and you undertake national and international driving work as directed by supervisor who is currently Dave Watson.
2. Your basic wages are £105 per week payable at fortnightly intervals and in cash.
3. Normal working hours will not exceed 40 hours per week. Extra working hours will be paid at time and a quarter and time and a half for weekend working.
4. Holidays will amount to four weeks per year plus public holidays.
5. For sickness allowance and payment procedures see the explanatory notes on the back.
6. Pension arrangements are described in the company's pension scheme booklet a copy of which is included in the envelope containing this statement.
7. Unless a serious breach of an employment term arises, notice of termination of employment is one month on either side, this not being a fixed term contract of employment.
8. Disciplinary arrangements are set out in the enclosed booklet entitled: 'Discipline at Humberside Heavy Haulage'.
9. If you wish to raise any grievance about the terms of your employment with the company please speak to Frank Fairbrother, Depot Manager, in the first place.

Notes (i) Any changes to these terms of employment will be posted on the noticeboard in Mr Fairbrother's office.

(ii) This statement is not your contract of employment which was set out in your formal letter of appointment and those terms and conditions implied by law.

Signed: Percy Proudfoot

Company Secretary

Dated: 13.10.86

Oral contracts

Oral terms in a contract of employment should not be ignored. In a recent case involving a driver of a heavy goods vehicle an oral promise was made by one of the driver's managers that the driver, a Mr Rump, would not be required to work anywhere in the UK, as mentioned in his contract of employment, but only in the south of England because of special family ties. The written terms specified: 'You may be required to transfer from one workplace to another on the instruction of the employer.' After five years' service, Mr Rump was ordered to work outside the south of England and, relying on his manager's promise, he refused. Mr Rump was not dismissed; he resigned, claiming constructive dismissal. The industrial tribunal decided that Mr Rump had been unfairly dismissed, that he was entitled to rely on his manager's promise and, accordingly, should receive compensation for such unfair dismissal.

Written contracts of employment

A written contract of employment should seek to cover all possible material points. It must, of course, include the details given in the written particulars which the employer is obliged to serve on the employee within 13 weeks of the start of his employment.

Under the Industrial Relations Code of Practice, paragraph 62, a contract can reasonably be expected to give information about:

(i) the requirements of his job and to whom he is directly responsible;

(ii) disciplinary rules and procedures and the types of

circumstances which can lead to suspension or dismissal;
(iii) trade union arrangements;
(iv) opportunities for promotion and any training necessary to achieve it;
 (v) social or welfare facilities;
(vi) fire prevention and safety and health rules;
(vii) any suggestion schemes.

To make the contract comprehensive, the following matters should also be dealt with:

- job mobility: will the employee be expected to move to another town if the employer wants him to work elsewhere?
- job flexibility: will the employee be expected to undertake different duties if required? If the contract contains a narrowly drawn job description the employee may refuse to change his duties.
- overtime: will the employee be required to undertake compulsory overtime?
- work rules: works rules and disciplinary codes will probably be implied terms. But to avoid doubt specific reference should be made in the written contract.
- restrictions on future employment: should there be a term restricting the employee's future choice of jobs (for instance, if he knows trade secrets or lists of customers)? Such a clause needs very careful drafting.

Employer's duties

An employer is obliged to provide a safe system of work and to pay his employees in accordance with the terms of their contracts.

Employers must acquaint employees of their rights under the employment protection laws, such as the right to maternity leave and the right to take time off for trade union activities (see below).

If an employer infringes the law, resulting in an employee being sued for this infringement, the employee can require the employer to pay any damages. In a 1951 case, a Mr Gregory was injured when a lorry driven by a Mr Hill knocked him off his motorbike. Mr Hill was driving in the course of his employment. Unfortunately, Mr Hill's employer had failed to insure the lorry. In a negligence suit brought against him Mr Hill wanted to sue his employer to indemnify him for the damages he had to pay out to Mr Gregory. It was held that an implied term of Mr Hill's employment contract required his employer to obey the law and insure the lorry. 'There was an implied term in the contract of service that the employer would comply with (the law) from which it would follow that the servant would be indemnified for any damage caused by his negligence.'

Surprisingly, perhaps, at common law an employer does not have to provide employees with actual work. If a lorry driver does not actually drive each day because business is slack, but receives his usual wages, he is not justified in complaining about lack of actual driving work.

An employer is not duty bound to provide a reference when an employee leaves. However, if a reference is provided, it must be a fair one.

Duties of employees

Employees must work to a reasonable standard, for the hours agreed. They must obey the instructions of their employer as long as those instructions are lawful; an order to drive an unsafe lorry would clearly have to be disregarded by a lorry driver.

Employees have a duty to take reasonable care in the performance of their duties. The well known case of Lister v Romford Ice & Cold Storage Co Ltd illustrates this point.

Romford's lorry driver negligently reversed his company's vehicle into another employee, in fact, his father. Romford's insurers paid the father's claim and then sued his son, the negligent lorry driver, to recover what they had paid out under the contract of insurance. The House of Lords decided that the lorry driver, as Romford's employee, owed his employer a duty to drive with reasonable care and skill.

Having involved his employer (under the concept of vicarious liability) by virtue of his negligent driving, the lorry driver was liable to Romford for breach of contract. The basis of this liability was to be found in an implied term in the lorry driver's employment contract to indemnify Romford for loss caused by his – the employee's – negligence. In such a case the damages would provide a complete indemnity for the monies paid out on behalf of the vicariously liable employer to the injured plaintiff.

While there is no general duty imposed by law upon employees to cooperate with their employer, they must not betray their employer's trust, for instance by giving away trade secrets.

Employee or subcontractor?

One of the features of the haulage industry in the 1980s has been the number of firms using subcontract hauliers who are owner-drivers. The question arises whether a subcontract owner-driver is really an independent contractor or, in fact, because he does so much work for a particular haulier, an employee of that haulier. The haulier needs to make a clear distinction, because if a driver is deemed in reality to be an employee, he is protected by the employment legislation. If, for example, the driver's national insurance contributions are paid partly by the haulier it may well be presumed that the driver is an employee.

Deciding whether a person is an employee rather than an independent contractor can prove extremely difficult. The 1979 Parsons case (quoted by Pritchard) gives some indication of judicial thinking on the matter:

> The three Parsons brothers inherited their father's haulage business and ran it, although most of the shares were owned by their mother. But the brothers argued and Leonard Parsons was voted off the board. He claimed unfair dismissal, but the company argued that he was not an employee and so he was not eligible. Although Leonard did not have a contract with the company, he was a director for life. Held: By looking at all the circumstances, it was clear that Leonard was self-employed. His pay was described as director emoluments and he paid tax and NI contributions as a self-employed person, thus he could not claim unfair dismissal.

Maternity leave

Under the Employment Act 1980 all pregnant women have the right to take time off work in order to receive antenatal care. Maternity pay – 90 per cent of the employee's usual wages for a six-week period – unfortunately does not come automatically. The claims procedure is very complicated, but once eligibility has been established, the employer is entitled to be reimbursed by the DHSS.

It is sensible personnel practice to have a standard letter available to employees which they can use to notify you of their situation and intentions. For example:

Dear Mr Dawson,

I would like to let you know that I am pregnant and anticipate my confinement will take place in the week before Christmas. As you know I should very much like to return to work in some secretarial capacity at Yorhaul Limited after my baby's birth and naturally wish to claim maternity pay, so please take this letter as formal notice of these matters as required under the Employment Protection (Consolidation) Act 1978.

You will appreciate that I shall need to take paid time off work for antenatal visits. The dates of these visits will be given to you as soon as they are to hand.

Perhaps you would kindly sign and return the enclosed copy of this letter by way of receipt.

Yours sincerely,

Pamela Forward
Secretary

Trade union activities

In the road haulage industry the trade union representative may have to travel to other regions in the country to coordinate practice and policy and should advise his employer of the importance of this type of work to avoid misunderstandings. Time off for carrying out trade union activities may require some interpretation. The Advisory, Conciliation and Arbitration Service (ACAS) has published a code of practice on this subject, 'Time off for Trade Union Duties and Activities', which is available from HMSO and other booksellers.

Injuries at work

In a fast moving haulage firm, great care has to be taken to provide a safe system of working; all employees should be responsible people who are 'up to the job', and all equipment and buildings used must be safe and free from apparent defects. This threefold duty imposed on the haulier at common law and by legislation, such as the Health and Safety at Work Act 1974, can be very onerous. Certainly a proper system of insurance to cover an employer's liability for accidents at work needs to go hand-in-hand with practical steps to reduce the likelihood of such accidents occurring. Overdrive, a company which offers hauliers the services of relief drivers to cope with peaks in their business, gives drivers specific job responsibilities under the 1974 Act (see the extract from their Drivers' Handbook below):

HEALTH AND SAFETY AT WORK ACT 1974

Specific job responsibilities
All drivers shall:
— at the commencement of each assignment, familiarise themselves with, and conform to, the client's health and safety programme at all times and undergo training where necessary.
— obey the client's safety rules and take reasonable care for their safety at all times.
— wear appropriate safety equipment and use appropriate safety devices as required by the client at all times.
— conform to all instructions given by the client's safety officer and others with a responsibility for health and safety.
— report all accidents and damage to both the appropriate client representative and the Overdrive supervisor whether persons are injured or not.

- not take any action which may endanger the health and safety of themselves, fellow workers or client employees.
- adhere to the rules relating to health and safety when working in an Overdrive office.
- report all potentially hazardous situations not recognised by the client's own health and safety policy to the designated client safety officer and the Overdrive supervisor as soon as possible.

Extract from Overdrive Drivers' Handbook

Advice on improving safety measures at a place of work is readily available from the Health and Safety Executive. The Factories Act, which covers garages and warehouses using mechanical power, as well as factories, has a number of detailed requirements. A local health and safety inspector may be glad to give you the benefit of his professional expertise on these exacting requirements.

If a major accident occurs at work, whether or not it is an employee who is injured, the employer should report the accident immediately to the local Health and Safety Executive officer, by telephone: written confirmation should be sent within seven days and a suitable entry made in the haulage firm's accident report book. A major incident which could have put people at risk, although, fortunately, no one was actually injured, must also be reported.

Anyone injured at work can obtain advice quickly from their local citizen's advice bureau.

Dismissal and redundancy

In the present economic climate, losing a job in the haulage industry can be very hard to bear. The haulier should take the greatest care in making sure his employees are fairly treated if their employment does come to an end.

An employer who wants to dismiss an employee must give proper notice. The minimum length of notice an employer must give an employee under Section 49 of the Employment Protection Act 1978 is one week when the employee has been employed between one month and two years. One extra week's notice has to be given in respect of each full year of employment up to 12 years. Twelve weeks notice is the correct period of notice for employment over 12 years.

The employee need not work out the period of notice if he prefers not to, although he loses his right to wages in lieu of notice.

An employer need not give any notice if the employee's conduct constitutes gross misconduct justifying instant dismissal. Similarly, if an employee cannot continue to work, because of an incapacitating illness, for example, no notice whatsoever is needed. But an employee not giving proper notice of termination of employment may be sued for damages by the employer. This is the wrongful dismissal claim in reverse.

An employer not giving an employee proper notice can be sued for damages for wrongful (not unfair) dismissal in the county court. Whereas a wrongful dismissal action covers a specific amount of wages, a claim for unfair dismissal covers general compensation by way of damages in respect of an employee's dismissal. On the question of giving an employee reasons for his dismissal, reasons need only be given if specifically requested by the employee (Section 58 of the 1978 Act).

A fixed-term contract naturally expires at the end of the contract period. If the employer or the employee dies, the contract of employment ends. So too if the employer becomes insolvent.

No attempt should be made to restrict an employee's future place of work by inserting a restraint-of-trade clause in the contract of employment. The courts do not like this sort of clause.

Unfair dismissal

An employee who is dismissed after two years' service has three months in which to complain to an industrial tribunal. He must show the tribunal that he has been 'dismissed'. The employer will then have to justify the dismissal. For this purpose the employer must show that he had a good reason for sacking the employee. It would be fair to sack the employee as incompetent or for being dishonest. The tribunal has to consider whether the employer acted reasonably in deciding to sack the employee. A certain and fair procedure has to be followed. If the tribunal decides that the dismissal was unfair then it has the power to order the employer to give the employee his old job back or to give him another job. Reinstatement is rare for obvious reasons; the employee receives cash compensation in most cases. The amount of compensation reflects the fact that he is out of work and compensates him for his losses. Compensation can be reduced if the employee's own conduct contributed to his dismissal. This is like the legal concept of contributory negligence.

An employer is entitled to dismiss an employee for misconduct. Poor timekeeping over a long period usually amounts to misconduct. Other fair reasons for dismissal would be misconduct in the form of disobeying the employer's orders, non-co-operation, causing violence, bad language, drunkenness, dishonesty, incompetence and incapacity.

Whether an employee is too ill to continue his job and should be transferred to another more suitable job or simply dismissed may be a very difficult question for the employer. It is suggested that the taking of medical advice and careful consultation with the employee concerned are essential before coming to a final decision on the matter.

On the question of reasonableness, an employer should have regard to the Code of Practice on disciplinary rules and procedures published by ACAS. A code of practice is not legally enforceable, like a statutory instrument, for example. But it provides guidelines as to what constitutes reasonable behaviour and it carries considerable weight at an industrial tribunal.

A sample paragraph (no. 14) from the Code of Practice states:

> When determining the disciplinary action to be taken the supervisor or manager should bear in mind the need to satisfy the test of reasonableness in all the circumstances. So far as possible, account should be taken of the employee's record and any other relevant factors. Whilst this code presents an ideal standard, the industrial tribunal will take account of the size and resources of an employer when determining the question of dismissal being reasonable or not.

Given that industrial tribunals hear most employment law

disputes, their procedure should be familiar to an employer. Explanatory leaflets are available from:

Secretary to the Tribunals,
Central Office of the Industrial Tribunals,
(England and Wales),
93 Ebury Bridge Road,
London SW1

The haulier certainly needs to be aware of the procedure on claims for unfair dismissal. A dismissed employee who makes a successful claim is eligible for a tax-free cash sum by way of compensation up to £4560 on a basic award and up to £8000 on a compensatory award. These awards are not alternative; different principles apply to their calculation.

Redundancy

Section 81 of the Employment Protection (Consolidation) Act 1978 states that redundancy occurs when:

- the firm closes
- the business is taken over
- the employee works less hours or is laid off
- the employee's work is reduced
- the firm moves.

In order to be eligible to receive a redundancy payment, a dismissed employee must show that:

- he was within the redundancy payments legislation
- he was indeed dismissed
- the reason for his dismissal was redundancy.

An employee needs to show that he has been in two years continuous employment. This is the same time qualification as that for an unfair dismissal claim. Dismissal may include constructive dismissal: the employer's behaviour proves so objectionable that the employee is obliged to leave. In other words the employer's conduct is so bad that a reasonable employee cannot be expected to endure it any longer. If the dismissed employee has been replaced by another employee this usually means redundancy.

Given that redundancy is a fair reason for dismissing an

employee, a redundant employee cannot usually claim unfair dismissal. This claim will succeed however if the employer can be shown to have behaved unreasonably. Giving as much advance warning of a possible redundancy, consulting with trade union representatives, selecting employees for redundancy using objective criteria and making sure alternative jobs are not ignored would show an industrial tribunal that an employer was acting reasonably. See case no. 1 outlined below. As most part-timers are women, it would be considered 'grossly discriminatory' to have 'a part-timers first' rule on redundancy selection!

If an employee refuses the offer of another identical job he loses redundancy entitlement. If the new job is different in any way, an employee can try it out for a trial period of up to four weeks.

For an example of how the amount of a redundancy payment is arrived at see case no. 2 outlined below.

Casenotes

1. *Redundancies fair because of union silence*

The continuing silence of the Transport and General Workers' Union over the selection of drivers for redundancy by Tarmac Roadstone Ltd on a quarry-by-quarry basis, resulted in a Nottingham industrial tribunal deciding that the company had acted fairly.

Three of the drivers concerned had argued that they had been unfairly selected for redundancy because there were drivers with less service who had been retained at other quarries. However, the company maintained that the redundancies had been carried out in accordance with an agreement with the union and therefore they were of necessity fair.

The tribunal was told that, following a review, the company decided to make redundant 16 drivers at the quarries it operated in the East Midlands. At Elvaston, where the three drivers concerned were employed, the whole of the transport fleet was to go. There was a meeting between senior management and union representatives, including the full-time district officer. Tarmac said that it would firstly call for volunteers, and to encourage volunteers it would make ex gratia payments exceeding the normal redundancy payment entitlement. If the number of volunteers exceeded the number required, the company would be prepared to move drivers from quarry to quarry to make up the numbers. However, it was emphasized that apart from that situation, each quarry would be regarded as a separate unit.

On all points apart from the last the union gave specific consent. To the last it raised no objection but it did point out that it might lead to long-serving drivers being made redundant whilst drivers with shorter service at other quarries were retained.

When the company indicated that it considered it was the fairest situation that could be achieved in the circumstances, the union representatives said that they noted the compnay's position.

The Elvaston drivers protested about the redundancies being on a quarry-by-quarry basis. When it subsequently became apparent that there were insufficient volunteers and compulsory redundancies would be necessary, the union was informed but there was no reaction. When the Elvaston drivers were made redundant there was still no protest from the union. The first that Tarmac knew that the union disapproved was when the present proceedings were commenced.

Holding that the dismissals were fair, the tribunal said that, whilst it accepted that the union did not specifically accept what was proposed by the company, it concluded that, by its continuing and sustained silence over a period of a month, the union had agreed to the compulsory redundancies being handled in the way the company had proposed.

Source: *Freight* August 1986

2. *Redundancy*

Peter Wilson aged 43, a married man with three children, has been employed by Humberside Heavy Haulage as a traffic clerk for five years and his current weekly wage is £120 per week. The company has seen haulage rates on some contracts in 1987 at little more than 1977 levels. The use of a new computer software distribution program calls for a reduction in manpower from three to two in the traffic clerks' office. As the last in, Peter Wilson becomes the natural choice to go first. Humberside Heavy Haulage Depot Manager, Frank Fairbrother, proposes to give Peter a week's notice and a terminal bonus of £250. Peter talks to his brother Alan who as the holder of a CPC (national) is aware of the basic workings of the redundancy payments scheme under current employment legisation.

Alan explains that his brother is entitled to at least five weeks' notice or seven weeks' pay 'in lieu' of notice, that is, £600. The Employment Protection (Consolidation) Act 1978 prescribes certain minimum periods of notice and Peter cannot be deprived of this protection no matter what Frank Fairbrother says.

The terminal bonus of £250, an ex gratia payment as a thank-you for five years' service, is painfully inadequate, advises Alan. Under the 1978 Act, which incorporates the terms of the Redundancy Payments Act 1965, redundancy may arise if the work needed to be done by an employee gets less or becomes unnecessary (in changed economic conditions) or is expected to diminish or come to an end. Peter, having been dismissed because his work as a traffic clerk has been largely supplanted by use of a computer program for traffic flows, vehicle scheduling and so on is eligible for a redundancy payment. Had he worked part-time as a traffic clerk or been employed for less than two years by Humberside Heavy Haulage, Peter would not have been entitled to a redundancy payment.

Alan confirms that the following formula would be used to work out Peter's redundancy entitlement as a full-time employee:

Given one week's pay due for each whole year's service from 22nd birthday to 41st birthday.

Given 1½ weeks' pay due for each whole year's service from 41st birthday to retirement.

Calculation as follows:

3 years at 1 week	= £360
2 years at 1½ weeks	= £360
Redundancy entitlement	= £720

Alan tells Peter that £720 is the minimum redundancy payment available. There is nothing to stop Humberside

Heavy Haulage from paying more than the legal minimum if the company really wishes to show appreciation of Peter's loyal service over the years.

3. The importance of law

The specialist contract hire firm, Overdrive, give a clear indication in their brochure of the importance of employment law for road transport operations. This extract from Overdrive's brochure is bound to impress a potential customer.

> Because the people who run our Overdrive offices are experienced, they know the legal constraints that abound in transport. All driver licences are inspected on interview and at least monthly thereafter; tachograph procedures are formally tested (and we issue a Manual to be safe); our drivers carry a Record of Hours Worked (to cope with changing Operators); we check out HASAWA requirements – we're both involved in that. Perhaps most important we fully employ our drivers and retain all employment responsibilities but they are under your direction and control under the Transport Acts.
>
> Better secure than sorry.
>
> Here's our driver, whom you may never have seen before; there's your vehicle plus its load which can add up to a pretty expensive package. How about a little security?
>
> * We scrupulously check references for at least the past five years working.
> * We operate a unique identity card, including photograph (so you know it's our driver and not a stand-in).
> * We accept liability for our driver's fidelity under clearly set out conditions which are easily amended for special circumstances (plus relevant insurances).
> * If despite all our care, things aren't right, we operate a 24 hour notification no-charge guarantee.
> * A different sort of security comes from our strict labour relations policy, regularly reviewed with the Unions plus absolute adherence to any site agreements.

4. Sex discrimination

In *Gunning v Mirror Group Newspapers Ltd* (1986 1 All ER 385) a young married woman was employed by her father (Mr Stark) in the wholesale distribution of Sunday newspapers to local newsagents. At one time the business ran five delivery vans. His distribution contract did not expressly provide for him to be personally involved in the distribution although his personal involvement was appreciated. On his retirement, Mirror Newspapers refused to give the contract for the distribution of their newspapers to Mr Stark's daughter, Mrs Gunning. A complaint was made to the industrial tribunal by Mrs Gunning that Mirror Newspapers had unlawfully discriminated against her in relation to 'employment' by refusing or deliberately omitting to offer her employment contrary to Section 6(1)(c) of the Sex Discrimination Act 1975. The case went on appeal to the Employment Appeal Tribunal and eventually to the Court of Appeal. The Court of Appeal held that as the main purpose of Mr Stark's contract had merely been the regular and efficient distribution of newspapers and since there was no evidence he should personally engage in distribution, it followed that the contract was not a 'contract personally to execute any work or labour' and therefore Mrs Gunning was not employed under such a contract. Accordingly, there was no discrimination against her in relation to 'employment' as defined in the 1975 Act. This meant that the industrial tribunal had no jurisdiction to hear her complaint.

Chapter 8
Obtaining Credit

Perhaps one of the least well understood aspects of trading is that of obtaining credit. People in business are often so pleased to obtain credit finance that they ignore the true nature of the obligations they have agreed to take on. Credit finance legislation is very detailed and complicated, and many lawyers are not competent to point out the basic pitfalls to unsuspecting clients. The best advice is to go to a specialist consumer credit/hire purchase lawyer for information on this very important matter. A selective glossary of terms relating to credit finance documents appears in Appendix 2.

The Consumer Credit Act 1974

The passing of a decade between the Royal Assent granted to the Consumer Credit Act 1974 (the 1974 Act) and the bringing into force of all sections of this piece of legislation on 19 May 1985 has substantially contributed to the general confusion. Lest it be thought that there is little help at hand, the Office of Fair Trading (OFT), responsible for much of the supervision of the 1974 Act, does supply some helpful explanatory material. Enquiries on the operation of the 1974 Act should be directed to:

Office of Fair Trading,
Field House,
Bream's Buildings,
London EC4A 1PR

Types of credit under the 1974 Act

There are four types of goods-related credit available, where the supplier of finance is also the creditor.

First, credit under a credit-sale agreement. If, for example, a haulage company wished to acquire a Volvo heavy goods vehicle as an addition to its existing mixed fleet of lorries, it would be given time – say, three years – to repay the sum borrowed, paying interest at a commercial rate each month for 36 months. The supplier of credit does not retain ownership.

Second, credit under a conditional sale agreement. In this case the supplier of credit does retain ownership while the monthly instalments on the Volvo truck are paid, usually until the very last instalment has been paid.

Third, credit under a hire-purchase agreement. This is very similar to a conditional sale agreement, the essential difference being that the hirer has the option to purchase the goods and is not obliged to do so. However, having paid all the instalments on the Volvo truck, it is hardly liklely that the haulage company would decide not to exercise this option.

Fourth, credit under a budget account. Instead of obtaining just one Volvo truck on credit, this type of arrangement allows the haulage company to purchase more than one item – say, three trucks – provided it keeps within the agreed (budget) limit under the credit agreement.

Classification of agreements

Under Section 10 (i) of the 1974 Act, running-account credit is distinguished from fixed-sum credit. A budget account is a good example of the former type of credit; credit-sale, conditional sale and hire purchase fall into the fixed-sum credit category.

Under Section 11 of the 1974 Act, a distinction is made between restricted-use and unrestricted-use credit. All the credit arrangements mentioned above are categorized as restricted-use credit.

The distinction contained in Sections 12 and 13 between debtor-creditor and debtor-creditor-supplier agreements is the one which causes most problems. Tim Sewell has written:

> I think it is helpful to think of the latter as debtor (creditor-supplier) agreements since this emphasizes the fact that in such agreements there is some connection between the

creditor and the supplier: either they are the same person eg in the credit-sale, conditional sale, or HP agreement; or there are business arrangements between them.

Regulated agreements

An agreement will only be regulated by the 1974 Act if it is not exempt. The debtor must be an individual, but this includes a partnership and a business organization which is not entirely incorporated. So a combined haulage operation comprising a partnership and company would qualify. The creditor may be any legal person including a corporation. The amount of credit must not be more than £15,000.

For a partnership wishing to purchase a new Ford van totally on credit terms under the 1974 Act, the following formula is applied to ascertain the maximum credit available:

Facts	Ford van total price=	£7500
	Deposit=	£1500
	Interest charges=	£1800
Formula	ADD deposit and interest=	£3300
	DEDUCT £3300 from total price=	£4200
	Therefore CREDIT=	£4200

Entering the agreement

A haulier taking up credit finance under the 1974 Act must sign a document in the prescribed form to comply with conditions laid down in the Consumer Credit (Agreements) Regulations 1983 as slightly amended by the Consumer Credit (Agreements) (Amendment) Regulations 1984. For example, the haulier has to sign inside the signature box personally. The creditor or his agent has to sign outside the box. Generally speaking, both signatures should be dated.

A clear example of an up-to-date hire-purchase agreement appears below, courtesy of the Consumer Credit Trade Association (Tennyson House, 159–163 Great Portland Street, London W1N 5TD). The CCTA can be contacted on 01-636 7564 for further advice on entering such an agreement.

HPM
(c)

HIRE-PURCHASE AGREEMENT
Regulated by the Consumer Credit Act 1974

These Documents are for Motor Vehicle transactions within the scope of the Consumer Credit Act 1974 signed on the dealer's or owner's business premises. The Hire-Purchase Agreement is to be found inside.

DEALER'S OFFER AND WARRANTY

To _____
Name of Finance Company

We offer to sell to you the goods, details of which are correctly set out in the attached agreement, at the cash price shown and in respect of such offer we hereby Declare and Warrant that:—
(1) the deposit shown in the agreement has been received by us in cash or by way of a proper and lawful allowance in part exchange,
(2) the agreement was completed in respect of all details before it was signed by the customer and we have complied with the provisions of all Statutes and Statutory Instruments affecting this transaction,
(3) the agreement was signed by the customer named herein at premises at which we or you carry on business and a copy thereof was then immediately handed to the customer,
(4) we are the holders of a valid licence as a credit broker under the Consumer Credit Act 1974,
(5) the goods are in a roadworthy condition and comply with the provisions of the Road Traffic Acts and all relevant regulations made thereunder. Where required a valid test certificate is held,

(6) the goods conform in all respects to any representations, descriptions, or stipulations which may have been made by us or our servants to you or to the customer or which may be implied,
(7) the customer has insured the goods under a fully comprehensive policy,
(8) we are not aware of any matter not fully disclosed herein which might affect your judgement in respect of this transaction,
(9) the goods are our absolute property, free from any lien or encumbrance, and have not been the subject of any previous transaction with the customer,
(10) any indemnity in respect of the agreement has been signed by the person whose name and address appears in it and such person has immediately been given a copy of it,
AND we agree that this offer shall only be accepted by your signing the Hire Purchase Agreement and that thereupon the property in the goods shall immediately pass to you and we will be responsible for giving possession of the goods to the customer.

Name of Dealer _____

Address _____

_____

Signature of or on
behalf of Dealer _____

Date _____

VAT No. _____

OBTAINING CREDIT

HIRE PURCHASE APPLICATION

Agreement No. _____

To_____
Name of Finance Company

I/We desire to enter into a Hire Purchase Agreement with you in respect of the goods described in the following proposed Agreement and make the following representations:

Surname _____
Block capitals
Forenames in full _____
Address_____
_____
Postcode_____
Phone No.
Home _____Business _____
Description of premises:
House/Flat/Furnished Rooms/Unfurnished Rooms
Delete inapplicable categories
Address occupied as: (give details, owner, tenant, with parents, etc.)

How long occupied? _____Years
Previous address (if less than three years at present address)
_____
_____
How long occupied?_____Years

Occupation _____
Business address or employers' name and address
_____
_____
_____
How long
_____so engaged? ___Years
Age_____Married/single _____
Number and ages of dependants_____
Bankers_____
Bankers' address _____
_____
Building Society _____
Building Society Address_____
_____
Current or previous vehicle credit transactions
Company Name _____
Account No._____

INSURANCE OF THE GOODS — Fully comprehensive cover required

Name and Address of Insurance Company or Branch Office _____
_____

Name and Address of Insurance Broker or Agent _____

Date of Policy or Cover Note _____ Policy or Cover Note No. _____

I/WE HEREBY DECLARE that the above statements and particulars are true and correct in every detail.

Date _____ 19_____ Signature of Applicant _____

BANKER'S ORDER FORM

I/We authorise you to debit to my/our account with you by Standing Order the undermentioned payments on the _____ day of each month for ___ months commencing on _____ 19___ for the credit of:

_____ at _____ Bank Plc
(Name of Finance Company) (Name of Bank of Finance Co.)
Account No. [ ][ ][ ][ ][ ][ ][ ][ ]
Branch Title _____
(not Address)
Sorting Code ___ — ___ — ___

Pounds / Pence
(in words)
and with the final payment an additional £ _____
(delete if not required)

(in figures)
_____ Payments of   £ / p
and a final payment of

To _____Bank Plc
_____
_____
_____

Signature(s) _____
Bank Account No. _____
Name(s) _____
(Block Capitals)
Address _____
Postcode _____ Date _____ 19___

When paying will Bank please quote Agreement No.

113

Hire-Purchase Agreement *regulated by the Consumer Credit Act 1974*   No._____

Motor vehicles — No right of cancellation

First Copy

This Hire Purchase Agreement sets out below and overleaf the terms on which we (the owners) agree to let and you (the customer) agree to hire the goods described below

The Owners _____VAT Reg. No. _____
Name and address

The Customer _____
Full names

Address_____

Particulars of the Goods		Financial Details	£	p
Make_____	Model _____	Cash Price of Goods		
Registration	Date First	(including £_____ VAT at_____%)		
No. _____	Reg'd. _____	Licence		
Chassis No. _____		= Total Cash Price		
Engine	Ign. Key	*Less:* Part Exchange £_____		
No. _____	No. _____	Cash £_____		
Body Type _____	c.c. _____	= Total Deposit (a)		
Colour_____	New or Used_____	= Amount of Credit		

Your Payments	Financial Details (cont)	£	p
Balance Payable to be paid by_____	Hire Purchase Charge £_____		
monthly payments of £_____	Option to purchase fee £_____		
commencing _____	= Total Charge for Credit		
and on the same day of each succeeding month	APR_____%		
	Balance Payable (b)		
(and a final payment of £ _____one month later)*	Total Amount Payable (a) + (b)		

* Delete if inapplicable.

TERMINATION: YOUR RIGHTS

You have a right to end this agreement. If you wish to do so, you should write to the person authorised to receive your payments. We will then be entitled to the return of the goods and to half the total amount payable under this agreement, that is £   .[1] If you have already paid at least this amount plus any overdue instalments, you will not have to pay any more, provided you have taken reasonable care of the goods.

1 Insert one half of the total amount payable.

Witness: Signature _____

Name _____
Block letters please

Address_____

_____

Witness: Signature _____
Second witness required in Scotland only

Name _____
Block letters please

Address_____

_____

Signature of (or on behalf of) Owners

_____

Date of Owners' Signature (Date of Agreement)

REPOSSESSION: YOUR RIGHTS

If you fail to keep to your side of this agreement but you have paid at least one third of the total amount payable under this agreement, that is £   ,[2] we may not take back the goods against your wishes unless we get a court order. (In Scotland, we may need to get a court order at any time.) If we do take them without your consent or a court order, you have the right to get back all the money you have paid under the agreement.

2 Insert one third of the total amount payable.

DECLARATION BY CUSTOMER

By signing this agreement you are declaring that:

★ You have carefully examined the goods and in your own judgement you agree that they are satisfactory and suitable for your purpose. This declaration does not affect your statutory rights.

★ Your particulars given to us are correct. You realise that we will place reliance on the information you have given us in deciding whether to enter into this agreement.

This is a Hire-Purchase Agreement regulated by the Consumer Credit Act 1974. Sign it only if you want to be legally bound by its terms.

Signature(s)
of Customer(s) _____

The goods will not become your property until you have made all the payments. You must not sell them before then.

TERMS OF THE AGREEMENT

1 Payment
Before signing this agreement you must have paid the deposit shown overleaf. By signing this agreement you agree to pay the Balance Payable by making the payments set out overleaf by their specified dates. Payments must be made to us at the address given overleaf or to any person or address notified by us in writing. Punctual payment is essential. If you pay by post you do so at your own risk.

2 Failure to pay on time
We have the right to charge interest at the APR (less that part attributable to any option fee) on all overdue amounts. This interest will be calculated on a daily basis from the date the amount falls due until it is received and will run both before and after any judgment.

3 Ownership of the goods
You will become the owner of the goods only after we have received all amounts payable under this agreement, including under Clauses 2 and 11, and any option to purchase fee shown overleaf. Until then the goods remain our property and your rights are solely those of a hirer.

4 Selling or disposing of the goods
You must keep the goods safely at your address and you may not sell or dispose of them or transfer your rights under this agreement. You may only part with the goods to have them repaired. You may not use the goods as security for any of your obligations.

5 Repair of the goods
You must keep the goods in good condition and repair at your own expense. You are responsible for all loss of or damage to them (except fair wear and tear) even if caused by acts or events outside your control. You must not allow a repairer or any other person to obtain a lien on or a right to retain the goods.

6 Change of address
You must immediately notify us in writing of any change of your address.

7. Inspection
You must allow us or our representative to inspect and test the goods at all reasonable times.

8 Insurance
You must keep the goods insured under a fully comprehensive policy of insurance at your own expense. You must notify us of any loss of or damage to the goods and hold any monies payable under the policy in trust for us. You irrevocably authorise us to collect the monies from the insurers. If a claim is made against the insurers we may at our absolute discretion conduct any negotiations and effect any settlement with the insurers and you agree to abide by such settlement.

9 Your right to end the agreement
You have the right to end this agreement as set out in the form 'Termination: Your Rights' overleaf. You must then at your own expense return to us the goods together with the registration document, road fund licence and test certificate.

10 Our right to end the agreement
We may end this agreement, after giving you written notice, if:
(a) you fail to keep to any of the terms of this agreement;
(b) you commit any act of bankruptcy or have a receiving, interim or bankruptcy order made against you or you petition for your own bankruptcy, or are served with a creditor's demand under the Insolvency Act 1986 or the Bankruptcy (Scotland) Act 1985, or make a formal composition or scheme with your creditors, or call a meeting of them.
(c) you make a formal composition with or call a meeting of your creditors;

(d) execution is levied or attempted against any of your assets or income or, in Scotland, your assets are poinded or your wages arrested;
(e) the landlord of the premises where the goods are kept threatens or takes any step to distrain on the goods or, in Scotland, exercises his right of hypothec over the goods;
(f) where you are a partnership, the partnership is dissolved;
(g) you have given false information in connection with your entry into this agreement;
(h) the goods are destroyed or the insurers treat a claim under the above policy on a total loss basis.

If we end this agreement then, subject to your rights as set out in the Form 'Repossession: Your Rights' overleaf, we may retake the goods. You will also then have to pay to us all overdue payments, and such further amount as is required to make up one half of the Total Amount Payable under this agreement. If you have failed to take reasonable care of the goods you may have to compensate us for this. You must also return to us the documents listed in Clause 9.

11 Expenses
You must repay on demand our expenses and legal costs for:
(a) finding your address if you change address without immediately informing us or finding the goods if they are not at the address given by you;
(b) taking steps (including court action) to recover the goods or to obtain payment for them.

12 Exclusion
(a) If you are dealing as consumer (as defined in the Unfair Contract Terms Act 1977) nothing in this agreement will affect your rights under the Supply of Goods (Implied Terms) Act 1973.
(b) In all other cases:
 (i) you rely on your own skill and judgement as to the quality of the goods and their fitness for their intended purpose;
 (ii) we will not be responsible for their quality, their fitness for any purpose or their correspondence with any description or specification.

13 General provisions
(a) The word 'goods' includes replacements, renewals and additions which we or you or the insurers may make to them with our consent.
(b) No relaxation or indulgence which we may extend to you shall affect our strict rights under this agreement.
(c) Where two or more of you are named as the customer, you jointly and severally accept the obligations under this agreement. This means that each of you can be held fully responsible under this agreement.
(d) We may transfer our rights under this agreement.

14 When this agreement takes effect
This agreement will only take effect if and when it is signed by us or our authorised representative.

IMPORTANT — YOU SHOULD READ THIS CAREFULLY
YOUR RIGHTS
The Consumer Credit Act 1974 covers this agreement and lays down certain requirements for your protection which must be satisfied when the agreement is made. If they are not, we cannot enforce the agreement against you without a court order.

The Act also gives you a number of rights. You have a right to settle this agreement at any time by giving notice in writing and paying off all amounts payable under the agreement which may be reduced by a rebate.

If you would like to know more about the protection and remedies provided under the Act, you should contact either your local Trading Standards Department or your nearest Citizens' Advice Bureau.

To be properly executed under the 1974 Act rules about the form and number of copies to be supplied have to be complied with. The Consumer Credit (Cancellation Notices and Copies of Documents) Regulations 1983 apply.

Terminating the agreement

The haulier may wish to make an early settlement of a consumer credit agreement, for example because he wishes to take advantage of a special seasonal discount being offered on a vehicle. To assist the haulier in making early settlement the creditor, upon receiving a written request, is obliged to give the haulier (the debtor) all the information he needs for this purpose. Full details appear in the Schedule to the Consumer Credit (Settlement Information) Regulations 1983.

Creditors are all too frequently obliged to terminate the consumer credit agreement because the debtor is in default. The case of Craggs and Citilend (see p. 133) shows a typical example. Perhaps the most practical advice is to contact a particular person at the creditor's premises and explain your financial difficulties. If these are genuine it may be possible to reschedule your debts under the agreement. The employees of a credit business will usually welcome your approach. The worst possible line is to ignore the arrears.

In conclusion, remember that consumer credit is a highly technical subject. If in doubt, take expert advice on your rights and liabilities.

Release from the agreement

Having made a credit agreement, it is usually not possible to cancel it. There are two important exceptions to this general rule. First, if the agreement is signed 'off trade premises' – somewhere other than a company finance office, showroom or shop – a five-day 'cooling-off period' is allowed. This period begins upon receipt by the debtor of a second posted copy, which has to be received within seven days of the signing of the first copy agreement. A letter of cancellation can be posted to the finance company within this five-day period.

Second, the finance company has to check the

creditworthiness of a customer from details supplied on a proposal form for credit, so it has the right to cancel the agreement at any time before credit has been approved and accepted.

Cancellation means that the credit agreement never existed.

Commercial credit over £15,000

As already mentioned, the Consumer Credit Act 1974 does not apply to credit transactions exceeding £15,000. The haulier should seek expert advice from one of the many financial advisers advertising their services in the press when credit over £15,000 is required. Without specialist financial advice, obtaining such a large amount of credit could prove foolhardy in the extreme. Since the 'Big Bang' in October 1986, the range of financial services has increased considerably.

Sources of finance

An overdraft facility at your local bank can prove extremely useful in meeting business expenses pending receipt of income from haulage contracts. A bank loan should not be undertaken lightly, especially if your bank manager wants security for the loan. Again, professional financial advice on the advantages and disadvantages of this form of borrowing seems a sensible precaution against financial embarrasment. Personal loans and credit card facilities are too well known to require detailed comment here. For the company wishing to borrow money, the company secretary should be in a position to advise (obviously with professional guidance) what borrowing powers the haulage company possesses. Every company has an implied power to borrow for purposes which are incidental to its business. A company's articles of association usually give powers of borrowing: 'the directors may exercise all the powers of the company to borrow money'. Article 80 gives a suitable general authority. All methods of borrowing open to individuals may be used by a company with the additional method of issuing a debenture.

Debentures

A debenture includes debenture stock, bonds and other securities of a company, whether amounting to a charge on the assets or not. It is a document which sets out the terms of a loan and is usually issued under authority of a company's seal. Repayment is provided for at some future date. Payment of interest is made to the debenture holder at a specified rate and at clearly defined intervals.

If a document resembles the form of a debenture although it is not called such, the usual rights and liabilities accrue to the holder. A debenture holder is not a member of the company and is entitled to interest on his debenture stock whether the company earns a profit in the accounting year or not.

A debenture may be fixed by a charge in the form of a mortgage covering specific assets of the company. Alternatively, the debenture may be secured by a floating charge, which has these essential characteristics:

1. It is a charge on a class of assets both present and future.
2. These assets change from time to time in the ordinary course of business.
3. A company is allowed to carry on business in the usual way until steps are taken to enforce the charge.

Particulars of charges created by debenture are kept at the Companies Registry and in the company's register of charges. The haulier should make sure that his company secretary keeps a proper record of debentures showing full particulars of company assets charged on the company's register.

Conclusion

Whether borrowing on a large scale or a small scale, competent professional financial advice is absolutely essential. Credit is a high-risk business. Suppliers of credit exact severe penalties if the borrower defaults. The haulier must be made aware of all the liabilities incurred under credit agreements.

Chapter 9
Debt Collection

It is common practice in the haulage industry to give customers 30 days from date of invoice in which to pay, and it must be the aim of every haulier to avoid giving extended credit to customers who, for one reason or another, fail to keep within these terms. At a time of economic recession and high interest rates this is a particular problem.

In keeping delayed payments to a minimum, the important thing is to have a simple routine which is operated as soon as a customer exceeds the credit terms given and accepted on the haulage contract. The routine for a haulier offering 30 days' credit might look like this:

Time	Action
31 days after invoice	Statement marked 'Overdue account – please pay immediately'
7 days later	Reminder saying, in red ink, 'Please pay now (not later) – this is a polite reminder accompanied by a copy of the haulier's ledger account
14 days later	Letter before action (see below)
10 days later	Proceedings

Of course, such a routine must be used with some flexibility. Telephone reminders are often appropriate and may be a good way of eliciting a genuine reason for any delay in payment. Regular customers who have paid promptly in the past often justify a special letter enquiring as to their reasons for non-payment of the current invoice. It may be worth pointing out to new customers who prove reluctant to pay on time that the keenly competitive rates being charged on the haulage contract can only be maintained if customers settle promptly. If a customer makes a part payment, the haulier should insist on immediate payment of the balance, pointing out, perhaps, the fairly small profit margins on which the business is run. If the haulier does not wish to be involved in the detailed process of debt collection he can always "sell" his debts at a discounted price or use a debt collection agency. Neither of these options is particularly cheap.

Letter before action

The aim of a letter before action (LBA) is to obtain payment from a slow payer without recourse to court proceedings. It has two essential components: identification of the debt and a clear statement that proceedings will be issued if payment is not made within a certain period, say ten days. In the example below, Haultech Ltd is owed £2950 by Datasystems of Newbury Ltd:

The Financial Director,
Datasystems of Newbury Ltd.
Bank Chambers
High Street, Newbury, Berks   19 May 1987

Dear Sir,
Re: Invoice 87/625
    Despite reminders, this account in respect of road transport services for £2950 (full particulars of which you have already received) remains unpaid.
    Unless we receive your remittance for £2950 within 10 days of today's date we shall issue proceedings against you without further notice or delay.

Yours faithfully,

Financial Controller
HLT

This form of LBA is well known to court registrars, so this letter can be sent on the firm's own notepaper, and there is no need to instruct solicitors to handle this stage of debt collection.
    When suing a limited company a formal company search should be made, preferably by law agents, to confirm the current address of the debtor company's registered office at which documents must be served. A search is the only way of

establishing the necessary particulars. Companies do some-times give incorrect details or omit them altogether on their company stationery.

When suing a debtor who is using a trade name without disclosing the names of the partners or proprietors of the firm, the LBA could usefully contain an extra paragraph:

> In accordance with Section 29 of the Companies Act 1982 we require you to provide us with the names and addresses of the partners in your business. We remind you that failure to supply a written notice immediately is an offence.

The debtor receiving a LBA may pay, do nothing or make some proposals about payment. If payment is received in response to the LBA, the haulier should acknowledge receipt and seriously consider whether he wishes to do further business with this reluctant payer. If no response is forthcoming from the debtor, the haulier should sue or instruct his solicitor to sue, as threatened. Any proposal to pay by instalment should only be accepted by the haulier if accompanied by some immediate payment; otherwise it has no value.

Court proceedings

If the debtor company does not respond to the LBA, court proceedings have to be issued in the appropriate court. Claims between £3000 and £5000 may be heard in either the High Court or the appropriate local county court. Claims over £5000 must proceed in the High Court. If the claim is within the £5000 limit, the local county court is usually the best option, particularly if the plaintiff intends to appear in person. In the High Court a limited company should instruct a solicitor to represent it. The local county court often has the advantage of being nearer than the High Court District Registry, its rules are less strict and it allows more steps to be taken by post than does the High Court. Court fees are also lower at the county level.

Some writers maintain that debt collecion through the courts is quite straightforward, and suitable for a litigant in person, but this writer feels that the case for taking advice and instructing a solicitor to conduct the debt action is very strong. If the LBA does not produce payment the haulier should send the papers to the company's solicitor. Instructions to sue can be given on a standard form with space reserved for any special comments. In this way the haulier spends as little time as possible on the matter and is free to get on with what he does best – haulage.

Those readers who would like to learn more about the art of collecting debts in person should look at *Taking Your Own Case to Court or Tribunal* by Edith Rudinger, from the Consumers' Association.

Enforcement of judgment

There are three stages to successful debt collection: identification of the bad debt, obtaining a court judgment against the debtor and thirdly, enforcement of the judgment. In practice enforcement can be difficult. Judgment can be enforced in the High Court by not dissimilar methods to those in the county court. (One method of enforcement is to have the action transferred to the county court for enforcement, by an attachment of earnings order.)

Enforcement in the High Court

The most usual form of enforcement is the issue of a writ of fieri facias (fi. fa.), which is very similar to a warrant of execution in the county court.

A form of praecipe (or request) for issuing of a writ of fi. fa. and the form of writ itself (obtainable from law stationers) should be completed and taken to the central office or to the district registry where judgment was entered, together with a sealed copy of the judgment and a fee of £6. The court office, after checking the documents, will seal the writ of fi. fa. and return it to you.

You should then send the writ of fi. fa. with a fee of £2.30 to the under sheriff for the county in which the writ is to be executed – that is, the county in which the defendant's assets which are to be seized are situated. (The addresses of under sheriffs are in the Law List, which should be at your local reference library). It is important to give the under sheriff as much information as possible about the debtor and any assets he may have, in the letter accompanying the writ of fi. fa. The under sheriff then issues a warrant for one of his bailiffs or officers to enforce the judgment by seizure of sufficient goods of the defendant to cover the judgment debt and costs, any accrued interest (from date of judgment to date of payment), the sheriff's charges, the fee on a writ of fi. fa. and the expenses of removal and sale. The under sheriff will acknowledge the writ and let you know which officer is dealing with the warrant; you should telephone the officer for reports of progress.

A visit by a sheriff's officer with a writ of fi. fa. may be sufficient to persuade the defendant to pay up, or at least make proposals to pay by substantial instalments. If not, the sheriff's officer will arrange for the removal and sale of sufficient of the defendant's assets. The sheriff's officer is entitled to deduct his own costs from the net proceeds of the sale. The under sheriff must hold on to the balance for 14 days in case any steps should be taken to make the defendant bankrupt, in which case he would have to pay the money he has recovered to the receiver. Otherwise, the under sheriff pays to the creditor sufficient money to cover the judgment debt, costs and interest and fi. fa. fee. Any surplus is paid to the defendant – unless the under sheriff knows of other writs of fi. fa. or county court warrants of execution, in which case he pays those off in date order.

If the execution is abortive, the creditor receives a bill from the sheriff's officer for work done (£15 to £35), and should insist on a full report about the debtor.

Enforcement in the county court

There are seven main methods of enforcing a county court judgment for non-payment of a debt. These are outlined below:

- inquiring into the debtor's means
- putting in the bailiff
- obtaining a charging order
- attaching the debtor's earnings
- obtaining a garnishee order
- petitioning for the debtor's bankruptcy
- obtaining an administration order.

The county court, often in the person of the chief clerk, will arrange for the debtor to attend for an oral examination as to his means. The debtor's answers are recorded and signed, becoming the basis of a realistic payment order by instalments in many cases. If the debtor refuses to attend for oral examination he is liable to be committed to prison for contempt of court. The creditor having instructed the court, the bailiff's officer asking on his behalf moves to distrain against the debtor's goods. The goods which are impounded are then sold off at auction and the proceeds of sale, less charges, paid over to the plaintiff.

If the debtor owns a property, the plaintiff can ask the court to make an order charging the debtor's house or flat with the amount of the debt. When the property is sold, the amount of the debt is paid to the plaintiff out of the proceeds of sale.

An attachment of earnings order requires a debtor's employer to deduct monies direct from the debtor's wage packet and pay off the debt over a period of months. The debtor cannot be left with a sum each week less than his protected earnings rate. This form of enforcement can be extremely effective.

Petitioning for bankruptcy tends to be the last resort, but even the threat of petitioning can prove most effective. The debt must exceed £750 for this procedure to be invoked.

An administration order is a means whereby the county court itself helps the debtor to organise his debts into a sensible order for payment. The debtor himself has to apply for this type of order, in practice often encouraged by the plaintiff.

Casenotes

Swannson-on-Wheels

Let us take the example of a debt owed to Swannson-on-Wheels for haulage carried out over a four-week period (throughout the United Kingdom) on behalf of a computer manufacturer called Computex Ltd. The family firm of Swannson-on-Wheels made a contract with Computex Ltd by exchange of correspondence. The following extract taken from a letter dated 30 July 1985 on Computex Ltd headed notepaper gives the essential terms of the haulage contract:

... I am therefore pleased to advise you that you have been given the contract for the delivery of 40 ZX Computex reader printers at £75 per drop, making a total charge of £3000. Deliveries of our new ZX machines are to be made during the month of August to one industrial customer at nine different locations throughout the United Kingdom, viz.

Exeter
Bridgend
Birmingham
Runcorn
Durham
East Kilbride
Lincoln
Norwich
Belfast

Collection will be made from our new warehouse in Corby, Northamptonshire. The order references for our machines are:

7531 : 10 lenses, 20 fiche carriers and 40 cartridges
7532 : 10 lenses, 10 fiche carriers
7533 : 20 lenses, 10 fiche carriers.

These order numbers have to be quoted to the warehouse superintendent, Pat Higgins, to obtain warehouse dispatch clearance for the machines. Each delivery drop comprises 1 ZX body, 1 lens, 1 cartridge and 1 fiche carrier.

I shall be on holiday during the last two weeks of August but if you have any queries during my absence on vacation my assistant, Jack Robinson, will answer these.

Yours sincerely,
Jim Dalliton,
Distribution Manager
Computex Ltd

PS I confirm our telephone conversation today when we agreed to make payment to you within 21 days of the last drop.

As agreed, Swannson-on-Wheels called to collect the ZX Computex machines and ancillary equipment from the new warehouse at Corby. Unfortunately, order number 7532 had not been met, due to problems best known to the Computex production engineer. Accordingly, the haulier had to endorse his receipt for the electronic goods 'items under order number 7532 missing'.

During the early part of August, the haulier completed all the deliveries to English locations, leaving Bridgend, East Kilbride and Belfast for the last two weeks of August. Some locations present special problems for the haulier, and Belfast is one of them, so this delivery was left until last.

In the absence of Jim Dalliton on holiday, Jack Robinson promised the haulier that, given the items under order number 7532 were still not available for collection from Corby, Computex would have to make separate arrangements for these items to be delivered. Jack Robinson wanted the haulier to complete the three remaining drops by the end of August as agreed. Adam Swannson, the senior partner of the haulage firm, confirmed these deliveries would be made on time, provided that he could subcontract the Belfast delivery. Jack Robinson thought this was a good idea but would have to check with his immediate boss.

The deliveries made to Bridgend and East Kilbride were short of items from order number 7532 but when the customer's branch accountants at each depot had this shortfall explained each was happy to take delivery and sign for the goods carried. The form of receipt was a simple endorsement on a copy of a letter sent by Swannson-on-Wheels to each branch of Computex Ltd's industrial customers giving notice of the scheduled delivery date for the reader printers, etc.

Despite the lack of a formal assurance from Jack Robinson's boss regarding the use of a Liverpool firm to effect the Belfast delivery, both Adam Swannson and Jack Robinson agreed this delivery could be subcontracted out. So, the final batch of Computex machines were delivered during the last week of August to the Liverpool subcontractor, who promised to deliver the ZX machines on or before the last day of August. In the event delivery was not made until early September and a strong letter of complaint from a dissatisfied Northern Ireland customer greeted Jim Dalliton upon his return from holiday. In these circumstances, the Computex distribution manager decided to withhold payment until he received a satisfactory explanation of the late delivery in Belfast.

In the event, despite attempts to settle the dispute in correspondence and on the telephone, the debt of £3000, exclusive of VAT, remained unpaid. A letter before action did not have the desired effect, and proceedings to recover the debt were started in the county court. Particulars of claim (with Swannson on Wheels as plaintiff and Computex Ltd as defendant) were drafted as follows:

PARTICULARS OF CLAIM

1. By letters dated 23 July and 30 July 1985 passing between the plaintiff and the defendant the defendant awarded the plaintiff a haulage contract for the delivery of 40 ZX Computer reader printers at an agreed total charge of £3000 (exclusive of VAT) such deliveries to be made at nine specified locations in the United Kingdom during August 1985 after collection from the defendant's warehouse in Corby, Northamptonshire.

2. It was a term of the said haulage contract that payment of the agreed price would be made within 21 days of the last of the nine deliveries. Due to circumstances beyond the control of the plaintiff the last delivery was made in early September rather than late August.

3. The plaintiff has invoiced the defendant accordingly full particulars of which have already been received by the defendant but the sum of £3000 (exclusive of VAT) remains due and unpaid.

   AND the plaintiff claims £3000 (etc.).

Having taken legal advice on the merits of the plaintiff's claim, the defendant decided to offer a settlement figure, with each party bearing their own legal costs, in order to avoid the expense of protracted litigation. The plaintiff, wishing to have monies now and not in two years' time, prudently accepted the settlement figure.

Smith & Jones (Contracts) Ltd

This case illustrates the fine line between debt collection and winding-up proceedings.

In June 1985 Robinson Bros Ltd, trading as Go Fast Transport (GFT), took on subcontract haulage work from Smith & Jones (Contracts) Ltd for five timed deliveries to a customer in Kings Lynn. The haulage contract was made on Smith & Jones standard form contract terms, endorsed with a special clause that in the event of any damage or delay to any of the goods, total payment would be suspended pending a satisfactory explanation as to damage or delay being received from GFT. The goods comprised 50 cartons of fragile machine parts to be collected from Tilbury, warehoused overnight at GFT's premises and delivered by 8 am the next day to catch the relevant sailing from the port of Kings Lynn. In the event two of the five timed deliveries were not made on time and the sailings were lost. Five of the 50 cartons were damaged and had to be returned to a workshop in Essex for repair.

Not surprisingly, given the terms of the haulage contract, Smith & Jones refused payment pending a full explanation from their subcontract hauliers. Bitter correspondence in July and August failed to resolve the dispute although Smith & Jones did make a without prejudice offer of £500 (in respect of the two deliveries which were made on time without damaged goods) to settle the matter. This offer failed to impress GFT and, having taken some informal advice from their company solicitors on winding-up procedures, instructed the local firm of Sam Sword and Spade, debt collectors, to serve a formal notice demanding payment of the outstanding £1250 (see below). Having received this notice of intention to wind up their company at Coldharbour Road, Smith & Jones once more offered £500, this time in an open letter, in full and final satisfaction of the claim for £1250, GFT having failed to provide a satisfactory explanation as to damage and delay. This offer was not accepted, the three weeks expired and instructions were given by GFT to their company solicitors to commence winding-up proceedings.

NOTICE

To: Smith & Jones (Contracts) Limited,
whose registered office is situate at
Coldharbour Road, Thames Marshes, Essex

WHEREAS (1) You are justly and truly indebted in the sum of £1250 to Robinson Bros Ltd trading as Go Fast Transport whose registered office is situate at Cornmarket Chambers Ipswich Suffolk more particularly in respect of transport costs for the quick delivery of fragile machine equipment and related warehousing costs

(2) By Section 517 (1)(f) of the Companies Act 1985 it is provided that a company may be wound up by the court if the company is unable to pay its debts (exceeding £750)

NOTICE IS HEREBY GIVEN to you pursuant to Section 518(1)(a) of the Companies Act 1985 that you are required to pay the said sum of £1250 to Go Fast Transport (GFT) not later than 3 weeks from tomorrow's date **AND** that if you neglect to pay the said sum or to secure or compound for it to the reasonable satisfaction of GFT an application will be made to the court for your winding up by petition presented by GFT under the provisions of Section 519 of the Companies Act 1985.

Dated this 10 day of October 1985
      Sam Sword & Spade
Debt Collectors of 2 New Place, Ipswich, Suffolk

Miss Fiona Fulsome of Pyramid Court, Middle Temple, settled a draft form of winding-up petition as instructed by these solicitors and their Derek Handyman duly presented the winding-up petition in the Companies Court Chancery Division High Court of Justice on 21 November 1985.

A copy of this petition endorsed with a hearing date for 13 January 1986 was then served on Smith & Jones at their registered office. After taking counsel's opinion, Smith & Jones' solicitors obtained a hearing before 13 January 1986 for a motion for the dismissal of this winding-up petition.

Before the hearing Smith & Jones paid GFT the £500 offered in correspondence explaining the balance of the £1250 was still in dispute.

At the hearing of this motion counsel for Smith & Jones argued that as there was a genuine dispute as to the sum of £750, it was an abuse of the process of the court to let the winding-up petition continue. A winding-up petition was not a suitable way to determine the validity of a disputed debt. Counsel referred to the case of Stonegate Securities Ltd v Gregory (1980) 1 All ER 241 at 243, per Buckley LJ:

> If the creditor petitions in respect of a debt which he claims to be presently due, and that claim is undisputed, the petition proceeds to hearing and adjudication in the normal way. But if the company in good faith and on substantial grounds disputes any liability in respect of the alleged debt, the petition will be dismissed or, if the matter is brought before a court before the petition is issued, its presentation will in normal circumstances be restrained. That is because a

winding-up petition is not a legitimate means of seeking to enforce payment of a debt which is bona fide disputed.

This argument was accepted by the court and GFT's petition dismissed given there was a bona fide dispute as to the balance owing of £750.

Chapter 10
Litigation

Going to court to resolve a dispute is rather like going to war. There are rules of procedure to be observed. Lawyers are usually required to prepare cases and defend them. The cost of litigation in the UK (unlike West Germany where fixed scales of charge exist) can be quite prohibitive. In this country civil litigation is based on what is called the adversarial system, and this means the court only decides issues presented by the parties. The court does not, of its own volition, enquire into the merits of the case. Most litigants have very little interest in the very technical procedural hoops which they have to go through – they are simply interested in the result. Litigation itself brings them face to face with the enormous differences between the theory and practice of law.

It is hardly surprising that any sensible businessman tries to keep out of court if at all possible. The costs involved in litigation are very high, and the delay in having a civil action heard in the High Court is often two years from the issue of a writ of summons. The advantages of trying to obtain an out-of-court settlement at a relatively early stage in the proceedings are therefore obvious.

If the matter does proceed to court, the stages of a typical contested action in the Queen's Bench Division (QBD) of the High Court include:

1. The issue and service of a writ of summons by the plaintiff upon the defendant
2. Return of acknowledgment of service form by the defendant
3. Service of the plaintiff's statement of claim, if not endorsed on the writ already
4. Service of the defence (putting forward the defendant's side of the case) and any counterclaim
5. Discovery of documents which have been or are in the

possession, power or custody of both plaintiff and defendant

6. Summons for directions for future conduct of the action
7. Technical preparations for trial, including collating evidence and taking proofs of evidence from witnesses
8. Attempts, if any, at settlement before trial
9. The trial (hearing) of the contested action
10. Judgment in favour of plaintiff or defendant and award of costs to the successful party.

The above stages should be clearly explained to the haulier by his lawyers so that a contested action does not become the sole preserve of the lawyers. A High Court action needs to be a team effort between the client and his solicitor and barrister, otherwise the action tends to run the client and not the other way round.

Commercial arbitration

The heavy costs and long delays involved in High Court litigation have led to an increasing use of some means of arbitration to resolve commercial disputes. The haulier should be aware of the basic advantages of this form of commercial dispute resolution. Privacy, relatively low costs, expert adjudicators, quick and relatively informal proceedings all make this form of determination quite attractive.

Expert adjudication on technical issues in the haulage industry will usually meet with approval from experienced goods vehicle operators who might be surprised at the lack of specific expertise in road haulage matters among the ranks of the judiciary. Judges are overworked and they are unfairly expected to show a very high degree of technical knowledge in some cases. Experienced specialist arbitrators are ideally suited to hear many more cases involving disputes over haulage contracts. Coupled with this expertise, lower costs make arbitration a very attractive option. Furthermore, arbitrations come to a hearing much quicker than ordinary court cases.

The control of arbitrations in England and Wales is covered

by the intricate provisions of the Arbitration Acts 1950, 1975 and 1979. The haulier interested in finding out more about the relevance of the arbitration procedure to his commercial disputes should refer to:

The Secretary
The Chartered Institute of Arbitrators
75 Cannon Street
London EC3

If the award of the arbitrator proves unreliable the court does have the power to set aside such an award. So, although the arbitration procedure is separate, it is under the ultimate supevision of the court to make sure that the system maintains high standards of adjudication.

Casenotes

The following selection of cases illustrates some of the most common kinds of lawsuit which a haulier might have to defend.

1. Citilend Ltd v Stuart Craggs provides an example of a case in which a haulier finds himself sued for a commercial misdemeanour – hire purchase default – in the Queen's Bench Division.

2. The case of Percy and Another v Smith illustrates the problem of keeping within the strict requirements of construction and use regulations.

3. Geldart v Brown and Others concerns the problem of complying with drivers' hours legislation (here the AETR rules, not the broadly similar EEC rules). The judgment on what constitutes an emergency for the purpose of deviating from the rules on drivers' hours merits close attention.

4. Orwell Transport's case concerns the tachograph regulations which are frequently infringed, deliberately and unwittingly. This case shows that real problems can arise even if an agent is specifically instructed to make tachochart analyses. The writer has great sympathy for hauliers confronting the intricacies of the tachograph legislation.

5. The Arctic Electronics case concerns the technical problems arising from an international road freighting

dispute involving subcontractors.
6. In Regina v Widdowson, a legal technicality saves the defendant – rather luckily – from a criminal indictment.

1. *Citilend Ltd v Stuart Craggs*

Set out here are

(a) notice of termination
(b) statement of claim
(c) defence and counterclaim.

> Citilend Limited,
> Citilend House,
> Tweedy Road,
> Bromley Kent

Mr S Craggs
t/a Craggs Haulage Contractors
Little Worsfield Farm
Nr Chelsfield, Kent

Dear Sir,

NOTICE OF TERMINATION OF HIRE PURCHASE AGREEMENT
TAKE NOTICE that we hereby terminate the hiring under the Hire Purchase Agreement dated the 4 May 1984 and made between this Company of the one part and yourself of the other part in respect of the goods specified in the Schedule hereto by reason of your breach non-performance and non-observance of the terms and conditions of the said Agreement.

TAKE FURTHER NOTICE that we hereby require you to surrender and deliver up the said goods forthwith to us or our Representatives.

SCHEDULE:

COMBI Truck   Reg. No. AMO 197A
H P Agreement No.   22/864321/02

Dated this 16 day of August 1984
Signed on behalf of Citilend Limited

. . . .
Designated Officer

IN THE HIGH COURT OF JUSTICE   1985-C-NO.3210

QUEEN'S BENCH DIVISION

B E T W E E N :

CITILEND LIMITED   <u>Plaintiff</u>

-AND-

STUART CRAGGS trading as

CRAGGS HAULAGE CONTRACTORS   <u>Defendant</u>

STATEMENT OF CLAIM

1.   By a written Hire Purchase Agreement Number 22/864321/02

(the Agreement) executed by the Defendant and dated 4 May 1984

the Plaintiff let on hire with an option to purchase one used

COMBI Truck registration number AMO 197A chassis number 0071

(the Truck) for a total cash price of £9500.   An initial

payment of £3500 was made before 4 May 1984 and the balance

due by 12 monthly instalments of £550 starting on 8 June 1984

was £6600 representing a rate of interest of 10 per cent per annum.

2.   The Agreement (to which the Plaintiff will refer to at

trial for its full terms and effect) required the Defendant to

pay the hire purchase monies on time and in full under Clause 3

failing which under Clause 7 the Plaintiff could terminate the

Agreement repossess the Truck and under Clause 8 claim such

monies from the Defendant as calculated in accordance with

the Citilend recovery formula full particulars of which

have already been supplied to the Defendant.

3.   The Truck was duly delivered to the Defendant. By 16 August

1984 the Defendant was 3 months in arrears.   The Defendant

was in clear breach of the Agreement having failed to make

any instalments at all.

4.   The Plaintiff treated the Agreement as repudiated by the Defendant and demanded delivery up of the Truck by a letter dated 16 August 1984. The Truck was repossessed and sold for £2000 plus VAT.

5.   (Alternative form of claim).

6.   By reason of the said breaches of contract the Plaintiff has suffered loss and damage as particularised hereunder.

(Particulars)

AND THE PLAINTIFFS CLAIM

(1)   Under paragraph 6

      (Particulars)

(2)   Interest pursuant to Section 35A of the Supreme Court Act 1981.

      (Particulars)

(3)   Further or other relief as may be just

(4)   Costs

HENRY ARCHER (Counsel)

Served this 9th day of September 1985 by

Ian Gunn & Company, Solicitors of

Bedford Row,

London W1

IN THE HIGH COURT OF JUSTICE   1985-C-NO.3210

QUEEN'S BENCH DIVISION

B E T W E E N :

CITILEND LIMITED   Plaintiff

-AND-

STUART CRAGGS trading as

CRAGGS HAULAGE CONTRACTORS   Defendant

DEFENCE   AND   COUNTERCLAIM

DEFENCE

1.   Paragraphs 1 and 2 of the Statement of Claim are admitted.

2.   Save that it is admitted that the Defendant had not paid
     any monthly instalments as alleged therein paragraph 3 of
     the Statement of Claim is denied.

3.   Save that the Defendant admits receipt of the Plaintiff's
     letter dated 16 August 1984 paragraph 4 of the Statement of
     Claim is denied.

4.   It was an implied term of the Agreement in order to make
     commercial sense that any sale of the COMBI Truck Reg No.
     AMO 197A pursuant to a valid repossession by the Plaintiff
     would be at a reasonable market price.

5.   In breach of the implied term recited the Plaintiff sold
     the Truck at a figure substantially less than the true
     market price. In May 1984 the Truck was purchased for
     £9500 and the vehicle was sold in February 1985 for
     only £2000 plus VAT. At the time of repossession by the
     Plaintiff the Truck was in excellent condition.

6.   The Defendant is entitled to a credit from the Plaintiff
     representing the difference between the true market

137

price and the price actually obtained for the Truck. The Defendant therefore counterclaims as set out below.

7.   By virtue of the above the Defendant denies that the Plaintiff is entitled to the relief claimed or any at all and paragraphs 5 and 6 of the Statement of Claim are denied accordingly.

8.   The Defendant furthermore is entitled to set off to reduce or extinguish the Plaintiff's claim the sums hereinafter counterclaimed.

COUNTERCLAIM

9.   Paragraphs 4 to 6 of the Defence are repeated.

10. Further and alternatively, the Defendant claims damages representing the reasonable market price of the Truck on repossession, or such other date as this court shall decide, less £2000 and less such sums as may be found due and owing to the Plaintiff herein.

AND the Defendant counterclaims:

(1) Damages

(2) Interest thereon pursuant to Section 35A of the Supreme Court Act 1981

(3) Such further or other relief as may be just and convenient

(4) Costs.

DAVID BOWMAN (Counsel)

Served this 3rd day of December 1985 by

Christopher Challenge & Company, Solicitors

of Crofton Road, Locks Bottom, Kent

Court decision

Having heard the evidence given by the parties, the court makes an order in favour of the plaintiff or the defendant depending on which evidence is preferred by the judge. Usually, the successful party is awarded legal costs against the loser.

On the facts presented in the pleadings, provided that the defendant could show some independent evidence that his COMBI truck was sold at an undervalue, he would probably succeed in his defence and counterclaim.

2. Percy and Another v Smith 1986 RTR 252

On appeal against conviction under the 1978 Construction and Use Regulations from the Humberside Justices sitting at Barton-upon-Humber, Stephen Brown LJ and Skinner J were asked to determine whether on the facts of the case a fork-lift truck, which had defective tyres and was being used on a road, was a motor vehicle for the purposes of the Road Traffic Act 1972. Section 190(1) of the RTA 1972 defines a motor vehicle as being within the Act if it is a 'mechanically propelled vehicle intended or adapted for use on roads'.

On the facts, the fork-lift truck was fitted with the following, according to the headnote of the Road Traffic Reports:

- a windscreen
- front and rear lamps (red to the rear and white to the front)
- flashing warning indicator lamps, both front and rear
- bodywork wings to cover the six wheels
- a rear view mirror in the cab
- a horn
- reversing lights
- brake lights
- number plates
- fork lift
- an enclosed glazed cab with two access doors
- bodywork panels to cover the engine.

The fork-lift truck was not fitted with either wing mirrors or a speedometer.

After an interesting review of the relevant case law, Skinner J cited with approval part of the judgment of Lord

Widgery CJ in Burns v Currell (1963) 2QB 433 and concluded his judgment:

> There was ample material on which the justices could reach the conclusion they did. In taking into account the user of the vehicle which they actually found or which they inferred from the practice of the previous owner it seems to me they did not err. They prefaced their findings by the statement that they applied the objective test to determine whether the vehicle was intended or adapted for use on public roads and they asked the question which was suggested by Lord Parker in Burns v Currell 1963 2QB 433,440. They were entitled in my judgment to take into account the actual use by the defendant company and the previous owner in determining what the ordinary use of that vehicle was on the road so far as it is relevant to the question they had to answer.
>
> In those circumstances the decision of the justices was right and I would dismiss the appeal.
> Stephen Brown LJ: I agree

3. Geldart v Brown and Others 1986 RTR 106

In this case the defendants, who owned two coaches making international journeys, were accused of contraventions of articles 6(2)(4) and 7 of the European Agreement concerning the work of Crews of Vehicles engaged in International Road Transport (AETR) and Section 96(11A) of the Transport Act 1968 as amended. As a defence to exceeding the normal drivers' hours of work, it was argued successfully, before the Kent Justices sitting at Sandwich, that these hours had to be departed from having regard to the care and comfort of the passengers. The defendants' actions were not detrimental to road safety and were exceptional cases as set out under article 11 of AETR.

The appeal ruling, which is just as relevant for the haulier as the PSV operator, confirmed the AETR agreement should be considered in the context of Section 95 of the Transport Act 1968. Section 95(1) provides:

> This Part of this Act shall have effect with a view to securing the observance of proper hours ... of work by persons engaged in the carriage of passengers or goods by

road and thereby protecting the public against the risks which arise in cases where the drivers of motor vehicles are suffering from fatigue.

The judgment continued thus:

In this particular case there was no detriment to road safety as matters turned out, but nonetheless that is the context in which these regulations must be considered. They are inevitably stringent, but for obvious reasons: because fatigued drivers are a potential danger both to other users of the road and to the passengers whom they carry. In order for the exception under article 11 to come into operation so as to relieve drivers and those who permit them to drive in excess of the hours which are prescribed there must be a real emergency. That was clearly not apparent on the facts of this case.

The appeal was therefore allowed, and the case was remitted to the justices with a direction to convict.

4. Orwell Transport

Operators who have their tachograph charts analysed by an outside agency need to be careful about exactly what it is they are buying and whether it meets their requirements in protecting them from breaches of the law by their employees and agents.

This warning was given by the Eastern Licensing Authority, Mr Kenneth Peter, when he considered taking action against the licence held by Orwell Transport Ltd of Ipswich, following the conviction of the company and one of its drivers on offences involving the falsification of tachograph charts.

In deciding to take no action against the licence, Mr Peter said that he bore in mind that it was due to be renewed shortly when he would want a report on the company's arrangements in regard to drivers' hours and records. It did not appear to be a case where there had been collusion between the employer and the driver to their mutual advantage. It was fair to say that, as soon as the company realized what was happening, it took prompt steps to rectify the situation.

However, it was well established in the field of goods vehicles operators licensing that if an operator relied upon an agent to perform functions for him, whether it be for the maintenance of vehicles, the checking of tachograph charts, or whatever, the operator must accept full responsibility for employing an efficient agent.

He did not know what was in the 'small print' of the contract between Orwell Transport and the tachograph analysis bureau that the company was using. He therefore did not know whether, if the contract had been carefully read, the company would have observed that the information provided from the analysis did not enable it to be notified of matters that needed investigation. For example, it might be that a driver was deliberately altering his records in some way. It appeared that it was possible to detect breaks in the trace similar to those in the present case, so the responsibility rested with Orwell Transport.

Warning that he would not be so lenient in the future, Mr Peter said it seemed to him that there was a warning for operators here generally, if they decided to go to a tachograph analysis agent.

The LA's message is an important reminder to operators, given the large number of tachograph analysis bureaux. Members using FTA's Freightcheck service can be assured that it is operated to the highest standards and specifically ensures compliance with the operator licence obligations.

Source: *Freight* August 1986

5. *Arctic Electronics Co (UK) Ltd v McGregor Sea & Air Services Ltd 1986 RTR 207*

Arctic employed McGregor to arrange for the carriage of 200 video game machines from Taiwan to Edinburgh. The Luxembourg air carrier Cargolux was employed by McGregor to bring the goods from Taiwan to Luxembourg Airport. Three firms of hauliers – Lies, Sortrai and the English firm Spa – brought the video games overland to London, where it was discovered that cartons from each load were damaged. Arctic sued McGregor. McGregor brought Cargolux into the proceedings as third party and for indemnity. Cargolux in turn brought in the three hauliers as fourth parties by serving fourth party notices on them. Lies contested the jurisdiction of the court. Cargolux maintained that Lies was one of the 'successive road carriers' under article 34 of the CMR Convention which provides:

If carriage governed by a single contract is performed by

successive road carriers, each of them shall be responsible for the performance of the whole operation . . . under the terms of the consignment note . . . .

Cargolux also asserted that Lies was one of the 'carriers concerned' for the purpose of article 39 paragraph 2 CMR which reads:

A carrier wishing to take proceedings to enforce his right of recovery may make his claim before the competent court . . . of the country in which one of the carriers concerned is ordinarily resident . . .

This meant that Cargolux could recover from Lies in England whatever the Luxembourg air carrier had to pay to McGregor or Arctic for damage suffered by cartons carried by Lies.

Cargolux argued that the Rules of the Supreme Court (Order 11) justified service upon Lies out of the jurisdiction, given Section 1 of the Carriage of Goods by Road Act 1965, article 34 and article 39 paragraph 2 CMR.

Lies applied by summons to set aside the fourth party notice served on them and succeeded in their application. It was held by Hobhouse J:

1. That the words 'carriers concerned' under paragraph 2 of article 39 CMR did not include a carrier claiming either for indemnity or contribution under article 37. (Article 37 provides that a carrier who has paid compensation in compliance with the provisions of this Convention, shall be entitled to recover . . . from the other carriers who have taken part in the carriage . . .)

   The Court of Appeal case of Cummins Engine Co Ltd v Davis Freight Forwarding (Hull) Ltd 1982, reported in Road Traffic Reports was applied.

2. That article 34 could not apply to the three hauliers on the simple reasoning that each carrier had a separate consignment note and article 34 only applied to cases where successive carriers operated under a single consignment note. Accordingly leave to serve Lies out of the jurisdiction could not be justified by Cargolux under article 39 CMR paragraph 2 and Order 11 of the Rules of the Supreme Court.

3. That as the Rules of the Supreme Court took effect

subject to any relevant statutory provision (in this case the Carriage of Goods by Road Act 1965), Cargolux having failed to make out their claim, leave to serve outside the jurisdiction had to be set aside as had all proceedings under the fourth party notice against Lies.

An application brought by Cargolux for leave to appeal against this unfavourable judgment was refused by Hobhouse J.

6. *Regina v Widdowson 1986 RTR 124*

Stanley Widdowson wanted to obtain a van from a garage on a hire purchase agreement. Knowing that his own name would not prove creditworthy, he inserted the name and address of a close neighbour on the standard proposal form which had to be completed to obtain the necessary credit. In due course, he was convicted, under Section 1(1) of the Criminal Attempts Act 1981, of attempting to obtain services, that is credit facilities for hire-purchase purposes, by deception.

Widdowson appealed against conviction on the technicality that obtaining hire-purchase did not amount to obtaining services. The appeal succeeded. It was held that when making a standard hire-purchase agreement, the hirer merely hired goods and did not obtain credit from the finance company. The hirer had an option to purchase on paying all the instalments and could terminate the agreement at any time. Accordingly, such a hire-purchase agreement could not be called credit facilities. Therefore on the facts of the case the indictment was bad and Widdowson's conviction had to be quashed.

Although not part of the actual judgment the court ruled that the obtaining of a hire-purchase agreement can amount to the obtaining of services by virtue of Section 1(2) of the Theft Act 1978.

Chapter 11

Insolvency

Insolvency is a very complicated subject. The latest piece of legislation on the subject – the Insolvency Act 1986 – is massive in scope and in length. It is described as:

> An Act to consolidate the enactments relating to company insolvency and winding up (including the winding up on companies that are not insolvent, and of unregistered companies); enactments relating to the insolvency and bankruptcy of individuals; and other enactments bearing on those two subject matters, including the functions and qualification of insolvency practitioners, the public administration of insolvency, the penalisation and redress of malpractice and wrongdoing, and the avoidance of certain transactions at an undervalue.

The parts of the statute are arranged in three groups. The first contains the following parts:

- I   Company voluntary arrangements
- II   Administration orders
- III Receivership
- IV Winding up of companies registered under the Companies Act
- V   Winding up of unregistered companies
- VI Miscellaneous provisions applying to companies which are insolvent or in liquidation
- VII Interpretation for first group of parts.

The second group contains the following parts:

- VIII Individual voluntary arrangements
- IX   Bankruptcy
- X   Individual solvency: general provisions
- XI   Interpretation for Parts VIII to X.

The third group of parts covers several matters of importance to the insolvency practitioner, but not of interest to the businessman.

The haulier should be aware of the circumstances in which he (or his debtor) may be wound up on a voluntary basis and the circumstances in which his company (or his debtor's) may be wound up by the court.

Winding up on a voluntary basis

The Insolvency Act 1986, Section 84(1), provides that a company may be wound up voluntarily:

(a) when the period (if any) fixed for the duration of the company by the articles expires, or the event (if any) occurs, on the occurrence of which the articles provide that the company is to be dissolved, and the company in general meeting has passed a resolution requiring it to be wound up voluntarily;

(b) if the company resolves by special resolution that it be wound up voluntarily;

(c) if the company resolves by extraordinary resolution to the effect that it cannot by reason of its liabilities continue its business and that it is advisable to wind up.

Once a voluntary resolution to wind up has been made, business must cease.

Winding up by the court

The Insolvency Act 1986, Section 122(1) provides that a company may be wound up by the court if:

(a) the company has by special resolution resolved that the company be wound up by the court;
(Provisions (b) and (c) relate to public companies.)

(d) the company does not commence its business within a year from its incorporation or suspends its business for a whole year;

(e) the number of members is reduced below two;

(f) the company is unable to pay its debts;

(g) the court is of the opinion that it is just and equitable that the company should be wound up.

Inability to pay

The definition of inability to pay debts should be etched on every businessman's mind. Section 123(1) of the Insolvency Act 1986 provides that a company is deemed unable to pay its debts if a creditor (by assignment or otherwise) to whom the company is indebted in a sum exceeding £750 then due has served on the company, by leaving it at the company's registered office, a written demand (in the prescribed form) requiring the company to pay the sum so due and the company has for three weeks thereafter neglected to pay the sum or to secure or compound for it to the reasonable satisfaction of the creditor. Section 123(1) confirms inability to pay if execution or other process issued on a judgment, decree or order of any court in favour of a creditor of the company is returned unsatisfied in whole or in part.

Two other ways in which a company is deemed unable to pay its debts must be mentioned:

1. If it is proved to the satisfaction of the court that the company is unable to pay its debts as they fall due (Section 123(1)(e)).
2. If it is proved to the satisfaction of the court that the value of the company's assets is less than the amount of its liabilities, taking into account its contingent and prospective liabilities (Section 123(2)).

Winding-up procedure

A winding-up petition may be presented by any creditor, amongst others (Section 124(1)).

Section 125(1) gives the court power to dismiss the petition, adjourn the winding-up petition hearing, make an interim order or any other order it thinks fit.

In case attempts are made to avoid the full effect of the winding-up procedure, Section 127 states:

> In a winding-up by the court, any disposition of the company's property and any transfer of shares, or alteration in the status of the company's members, made after the commencement of the winding-up is, unless the court otherwise orders, void.

Except in cases where the winding-up is voluntary, the

procedure starts with the presentation of the petition. In voluntary cases, the winding-up procedure starts when the necessary resolution for winding up is passed by the directors of the insolvent company.

Bankruptcy

Under Section 264(1) a petition for a bankruptcy order to be made against an individual may be brought by a creditor or by the individual himself, amongst others.

A bankruptcy petition, put before the court and registered on the court file, cannot be withdrawn without the court's permission, so presentation of this kind of application should not be undertaken lightly. When presenting his petition, a creditor should be owed a sum equal to or exceeding what is known as the bankruptcy level. The present bankruptcy level is £750, the same figure referred to in the company winding-up procedure above.

If an individual appears unable to pay his debts or has no reasonable prospect of paying he may also face a bankruptcy petition. Section 268 gives a definition of inability to pay which is similar to that for companies referred to above.

The court will not make a bankruptcy order unless it is satisfied that the individual cannot pay his debts. Section 271(3) provides:

> The court may dismiss the petition if it is satisfied that the debtor is able to pay all his debts or is satisfied
> (a) that the debtor has made an offer to secure or compound for a debt in respect of which the petition is presented,
> (b) that the acceptance of that offer would have required the dismissal of the petition, and
> (c) that the offer has been unreasonably refused.

Sections 272 to 275 cover the procedure to be followed on a debtor's petition, including the interesting role of the insolvency practitioner.

Professional advice

The Insolvency Act 1986, which became law on 29 December 1986, brings about the greatest changes in bankruptcy law and practice for more than a century. The familiar Bankruptcy Act 1914 has gone, and concepts such as acts of bankruptcy, adjudication and the receiving order will disappear. An entirely new form of money claim, called a 'statutory demand' (which does not have to be based upon a judgment) may revolutionize debt-collecting and litigation procedures.

Such dramatic changes in the law make the need for expert guidance in matters of corporate and personal insolvency essential. The haulier should look for an insolvency practitioner able to give up-to-date and detailed advice in accordance with the new law. A list of insolvency practitioners (ie solicitors with special expertise in the field of insolvency and approved as such) may be referred to at the Law Society's Hall, 113 Chancery Lane, London WC2A 1PL (Tel: 01–242 1222). Under the new Publicity Code for Solicitors (operative from 1 February 1987), solicitors may advertize particular interests, such as insolvency law, in various types of media. The haulier should not, therefore, have any great difficulty in finding expert help on insolvency matters from the right quarters.

Chapter 12
Expanding the Haulage Business

Small firms service

Without rigorous financial controls, a haulier will never find himself in the happy position of considering a real expansion of his business. It cannot be stressed enough that an adequate system for financial control must be a priority matter for the haulier. Having adopted good financial control procedures, the haulier will be in a position to expand business activities and establish depots in other parts of the country. A family business, with quite modest funds, has a pressing need for more capital. A capital injection from the company's bank has to be looked at as a probable source of additional finance, although this would mean a secured loan. Most directors would like to keep the company's business premises free from further encumbrances if at all possible.

For the projected sales and costs (budget) in the forth-coming year, which need to be drawn up whether or not they are used for obtaining bank finance, the haulier could use the profit-and-loss budget form recommended by the Small Firms Service of the Department of Trade and Industry (see below).

Franchising

According to the British Franchise Association (BFA), franchising is the method by which the owner of a business (franchisor) contractually agrees to allow another independent person or company (franchisee) to market a certain product or service within a specified geographical area. For his part, the franchisee makes a payment to the franchisor for the rights to a particular area and a royalty based upon sales expressed as a percentage of sales.

Form recommended by the Small Firms Service of the DTI

Profit-and-loss budget form . . . . prepared by

. . . . date . . . .

Name of business . . . .

Period, from . . . . to . . . .

(weekly/monthly/quarterly/half-yearly/annual)

	Budget £	Actual £
Sales (number of units . . . .)		
Other receipts	. . . .	. . . .

Direct costs:-	Budget £	Actual £
Labour		
Materials		
Total direct costs	. . . .	. . . .

Gross profit . . . .

Overheads	Budget	Actual
Rent		
Rates		
Water rates		
Insurances		
Repairs		
Maintenance		
Alterations		
Admin. salaries		
Sales salaries		
Cars		
Travelling		
Publicity		
Printing		
Stationery		
Postage		
Telephone and telex		
Consumable stores		
Tools and equipment		
Packaging		
Delivery		
Professional fees		
Bank charges		
Interest on borrowing		
Loan repayments		
Etc		

Total	. . . .	. . . .

Profit and loss pre-tax . . . .

Payments for tax (seek advice about tax provision in due course)

EXPANDING THE HAULAGE BUSINESS

There are three main types of franchise: job, business format and investment franchise. A job franchise in the haulage industry would typically be such that the franchise would invest in a lorry and anticipate an income closely allied to driving hours undertaken. A business format franchise is typically operated from a shop or restaurant. (The British School of Motoring is an example.) An investment franchise, as the name suggests, does not offer daily earnings, but rather a return on a profitable investment.

For many hauliers the idea of obtaining additional capital by way of a franchise payment is very appealing. Let us take as an example a haulage company which has acquired certain specialist expertise in transporting hi-tech products for companies based in North Yorkshire. This company would now like to expand its area of operation by establishing franchisee hauliers in other parts of the north of England. The relatively high levels of unemployment and redundancy payments in the north are important factors to consider. A job franchise as a haulier might well be an attractive proposition to a man on the dole, with a modest redundancy payment, keen to work again in the road transport industry.

A recent BFA survey showed that London and the home counties account for almost half the franchises in the country. All the more reason perhaps to increase the franchising activity north of Watford. Franchising is the fastest growing sector in the small business world. While a franchise means forfeiting some independence, the franchisee does receive the protection and active support of a sound and profitable business organization.

Anyone wishing to take on a franchise can ask the BFA for help and advice:

Franchise Chambers,
75A Bell Street,
Henley on Thames,
Oxfordshire, RG9 2BD
Tel: 0491 578049

Job franchising in the characteristically small business world of haulage contracting may prove very successful. The franchising industry has over 110,000 people in direct employment, and a sales figure (at today's prices) of £5 billion a year projected for 1990. Expanding haulage firms, however, seem largely to have neglected the possibilities offered by a franchising arrangement. Perhaps the rest of the decade will see greater use being made of this popular business device for raising capital for the franchisor and creating work for the franchisee.

Contract hire

The idea of using contract hire to increase the number of lorries in the fleet without a huge outflow of capital reserves deserves careful consideration. Many hauliers have spent years operating vehicles actually owned by the haulage company, but the benefits of expanding business using some form of contract hire agreement cannot be ignored. The advantages of hiring lorries on contract are set out below:

1. The operation of your commercial fleet at a known and predetermined cost per annum allowing a much more realistic vehicle budget to be met.
2. Releases money currently tied up in a depreciating asset on which no direct return is being obtained or capital employed. This capital could be used for the furtherance of your main business interests.
3. A higher standard of vehicle maintenance and repair resulting in a more efficient fleet.
4. Substitute vehicles available enabling you to maintain a consistently high standard of delivery service to your customers.
5. Care of all administration, DOE paperwork and records etc, thus freeing management time for alternative work.
6. Vehicles cleaned and maintained on a programmed schedule giving a good company image at all times.
7. Contract hire charges are revenue expenditure – therefore qualifying for 100 per cent tax benefits.

Note: A full maintenance programme would cover:
- all routine maintenance
- spare parts
- tyres
- MOT preparation and test
- monthly DOE inspections
- road fund licence

- repainting of vehicle during the contract life
- vehicle washing
- all relevant ministry paperwork and records etc.

(List based on a Ryder Truck Rental quotation)

European haulage

Most haulage businesses will probably look carefully at the prospects in Europe when reviewing new market potential.

The CPC (International) is a necessary qualification for European haulage operations. (*A Study Manual of Professional Competence in Road Transport Management* by David Lowe provides an excellent comprehensive course of study for this important qualification.) The syllabus covers the following subjects:

- law
- access to the market
- customs, practice and formalities
- operations, technical standards and road safety.

The section on law covers EEC driving hours regulations (EEC Regulation 543/69 as amended). On 29 September 1986 significant changes were made to these regulations with a view to providing a more liberal regime for drivers in Europe. The new rules are set out below. It is hoped that under pressure from the IRU, the RHA and the FTA, further improvements will be made to bring legal rules closer to sensible practice in the highly competitive international freighting market.

Apart from the subject of drivers' hours, the rules relating to the fitment and use of tachographs on European journeys need to be thoroughly understood. The rules are almost the same as for domestic operations. The main difference is that there is no need to note when daily duty (in contrast to daily driving) starts and ends.

Drivers subject to the EEC rules

Maximum period before break must be taken	4.5 hours accumulated driving
Minimum length of break	45 minutes

Maximum daily driving	9 hours (10 hours twice a week – all vehicles)
Maximum daily duty	No specific limit but controlled through daily rest provision
Minimum daily rest	11 hours reducible to 9 hours three times a week – reduction to be compensated
Maximum weekly driving	Weekly rest must be taken after 6 daily driving periods
Maximum fortnightly driving	90 hours
Maximum weekly duty	No specific limit but controlled by weekly rest provision
Minimum weekly rest	45 hours – reducible with compensation
The week	Fixed – 00.00 hours Monday to 24.00 hours Sunday

Drivers exempted from the EEC rules

Maximum daily driving	10 hours
Maximum daily duty	11 hours
Maximum continuous duty	Abolished
Maximum daily spreadover	Abolished
Minimum length of break	Abolished
Minimum daily rest	Abolished
Maximum weekly duty	Abolished
Minimum weekly rest	Abolished

Source: Freight, September 1986

Customs 88

The haulage business can easily overlap into an area which has been jealously guarded by the freight forwarding fraternity, namely international documentation. The advent of Customs 88 provides an ideal opportunity for the haulier to become more aware of this fascinating area of business.

As explained in the FTA's *International Digest* (Comment, 9/86):

> The revolution in customs procedures timed for 1 January 1988 will affect every UK company involved in international trade. No company, irrespective of its size, can afford to ignore these changes. Equally, no company should fail to take advance action to prepare itself for them.
>
> Early in 1985 FTA began discussions with representatives from Customs & Excise on the range of issues that have come to be known as Customs 88. The impending changes arise from a worldwide desire to streamline and standardize international trading procedures. The overall objective of these measures is to facilitate trade. The changes range from the introduction of the Single Administrative Document to a new worldwide tariff nomenclature and a new much enhanced customs entry processing system.
>
> The effect of these changes will be far-reaching and transport will, in many respects, be at the sharp end. The importance of adequate preparation cannot be over-emphasized in view of the substantial delays and costs that could arise through error.

Every haulier, wittingly or otherwise, will become involved to some extent in Customs 88 procedures. The best course must be to acquire some expertise in the procedures; not only will this be useful in itself, but the knowledgeable haulier may find others in the business who are willing to pay for help on Customs 88 documentation.

The distinction between a haulage company and a freight forwarding company with its own road haulage arm is rather blurred at present. Customs 88 may create a further blurring of the division, to the clear advantage of those hauliers prepared to expand business activities into the paperwork jungle of international trade documentation.

Specialization

The days of general haulage operations on a small scale are long past. Most haulage contractors are not able to make the economies of scale which are necessary to make general haulage profitable, and their obvious need is to specialize.

Dangerous goods and perishable goods are two examples of operational specializations worth serious consideration. In the case of dangerous goods, there are complicated and frequently changing regulations on classification, labelling and packing, but the rewards make expansion into this specialist area of operation extremely worthwhile.

The entry of Spain and Portugal to the EEC has resulted in more perishable goods being imports into the UK. This may be an opportunity for some British haulage companies to expand their business.

Section 8 grants

A road haulage business seeking to expand need not restrict itself entirely to the road transport industry. There is a growing awareness of the opportunities for hauliers presented by part ownership of private railway sidings. Government grants, up to 50 per cent of capital investment, make it possible for a syndicate of small haulage contractors to collect goods, carried long-distance by rail, for further distribution by road.

> Section 8 of the Railways Act 1974 allows grant payments to be made to suitable applicants, provided that there will be a significant environmental benefit, the anticipated expenditure is of a capital not revenue nature, British Rail will carry the desired freight, the rail freight facilities will encourage a transfer from road to rail and that, relatively speaking, the wanted rail freight facilities would not be viable without a Section 8 payment.
>
> Deanside Transit Limited, based near Glasgow city centre, is a recent example of a successful applicant for a Section 8 grant, now undertaking a sizeable rail/road transhipment operation. This Scottish storage and distribution firm presently receives five trains daily carrying over 1500 tonnes of freight. Deanside's sister haulage company, John G Russell, with a main operating centre at Gartcosh, has greatly improved its transport of coal operations with the benefit of Section 8 grant monies.
> (Freight, October 1986)

Integrated distribution systems

A natural development for the haulier in the 1980s is the use of an integrated distribution system. A prime example of this type of system is run by Freight Computer Systems, part of the National Freight Consortium, Europe's largest transport and distribution company. This distribution management, called Genesis, comprises seven modules:

- sales order processing
- stock control and order picking
- warehousing
- purchase order processing
- financial systems
- fleet management
- management reporting.

Currently supporting over 400 companies in the UK, FCS has been designing and putting into operation distribution systems for over 12 years. The idea of Genesis is to help managers operate more efficiently in the highly competitive transport and distribution industry. It aims to do this particularly by cutting down administration costs and releasing management time for more valuable tasks than ploughing through mountains of paperwork.

Managing legal rules

Expansion of a haulage business, even with the aid of computer-based distribution management techniques, inevitably means coming to terms with more rules of law. The progressive haulier is therefore well advised to give one manager, perferably a senior one with a thorough under-standing of his company's main problems in complying with the law, responsibility for 'managing legal rules'. Backed up by good professional advice, this form of management creates an active approach towards legal matters.

A concise report could be made available every month to all managers in the firm. This report would highlight important changes in the law likely to affect haulage operations in the short and medium term. Ample time should be made available to discuss such matters. Putting 'managing legal rules' high on the agenda of management meetings helps to achieve this objective. With this kind of monthly reporting, the common negative reactions to the welter of transport legislation can be replaced by far more useful and positive attitudes.

At a time when members of the legal profession in this country are beginning to appreciate management techniques, the haulage industry could usefully take more account of the impact of the law.

Appendix 1

Green Card Bureaux

NAME AND ADDRESSES OF BUREAUX

A	AUSTRIA	VERBAND der, VERSICHERUNGSUNTERNEHMUNGEN OSTERREICHS, Schwarzenbergplatz 7, Postfach 191, A-1031 Wien. Tel: (0222) 75.76.51-0.
B	BELGIUM	BUREAU BELGE des ASSUREURS AUTOMOBILES Maison de l'Assurance, Square de Meeus, 29, B/1040 Bruxelles. Tel: 02/513.68.45.
BG	BULGARIA	'BULSTRAD' BULGARIAN FOREIGN INSURANCE & REINSURANCE CO LTD, 5 Dunav Street, Sofia. Tel: 85191.
CS	CZECHOSLOVAKIA	BUREAU OF COMPULSORY INSURANCE FOR THE TERRITORY OF CSSR, Spalena 14/16, 114 00 Praha 1, Czechoslovakia. Tel: 2148111/298641.
DK	DENMARK	DANSK FORENING FOR INTERNATIONAL MOTORKØRETØJS FORSIKRING, Amaliegade 10, 1256 København K, Tel: 01-13 7555.
SF	FINLAND	LIIKENNEVAKUUTUSYHDISTYS, Bulevardi 28, SF-00120 Helsinki 12. Tel: 19251.
F	FRANCE	BUREAU CENTRAL FRANCAIS, 118 Rue de Tocqueville, 75850 Paris (17 eme). Tel: 766.52.64.
DDR	GERMAN, Democratic Republic	STAATLICHE VERSICHERUNG der Deutschen Demokratischen Republik, Buro fur Kraftfahrzeugschaden, Wichertstrasse 68, DDR 1071 Berlin. Tel: 4491 081.
D	GERMANY, Federal Republic	HUK-VERBAND, Postfach 10 63 03, Glockengiesserwall 1, 2 Hamburg 1, Tel: (040) 32 1071.
GB	GREAT BRITAIN & NORTHERN IRELAND	MOTOR INSURERS' BUREAU, Aldermary House, Queen Street, London, EC4N 1TR. Tel: 01-248 4477.
GR	GREECE	MOTOR INSURERS' BUREAU, c/o Association of Insurance Companies operating in Greece, 10 Xenofontos Street, Athens 118. Tel: 323.6733.
H	HUNGARY	ÁLLAMÍ BIZTOSÍTÓ, Insurance Enterprise of the State, 1990 Budapest, XIV, Gvadanyi UT 69. Tel: 835-350.
IS	ICELAND	ALPJÓDLEGAR BIFREIDATRYGGINGAR Á ÍSLANDI. International Motor Insurance in Iceland, Sudurlandsbraut 6 105 Reykjavik. Tel: 81612.
IR	IRAN	GREEN CARD BUREAU OF IRAN c/o Bimeh Markazi Iran, 149, Ayatollah Taleghani Avenue, Tehran. Tel: 649912 – 649913 – 649865 – 649875 – 649870 – 649715 – 649716.
IRQ	IRAQ	NATIONAL INSURANCE COMPANY Khullani St., P.O. Box 248, Al Aman Bldg., Bagdad, Iraq. Tel: 68521-10, 8875929, 8876857.

IRL	IRELAND Republic of	IRISH VISITING MOTORISTS' BUREAU LTD., 5/9 South Frederick Street, Dublin 2. Tel: Dublin 719443, 774569.
IL	ISRAEL	ISRAEL INSURANCE ASSOCIATION, THE GREEN CARD BUREAU, 39 Rothschild Boulevard, P.O.B. 2622, Tel Aviv. Tel: 03-627333.
I	ITALY	UFFICIO CENTRALE ITALIANO (U.C.I.) Soc. Cons. arl 20121 Milano, Corso Venezia. 8, Tel: 709.683, 798.278, or 709843, 781891.
L	LUXEMBOURG	BUREAU LUXEMBOURGEOIS des Assurers, 3 Rue Guido Oppenheim, Boite Postale 1772, 1017-Luxembourg. Tel: 4421 44.
MA	MOROCCO	BUREAU CENTRAL MAROCAIN, 300 Rue Mostafa El Maani, Casablanca. Tel: 2684-15.
NL	NETHERLANDS	NEDERLANDS BUREAU DER MOTORRIJTUIGVERZEKE-RAARS, Groot Hertoginnelaan 8, 2517 EG's-Gravenhage. Tel: 070-614731.
N	NORWAY	TRAFIKKORISKRINGSFORENIGEN. Hansteens Gate 2, Postboks 2551. Solli, Oslo 2. Tel: 56-66-90.
PL	POLAND	WARTA, Insurance and Reinsurance Co Ltd, Branch Office 00-010 Warszawa, ul, Chalubinskiego 8. Tel: 30-03-34.
P	PORTUGAL	ASSOCIACAO PORTUGUESA DE SEGUROS, Ave José Malhoa Lote 1674-1. 1000 Lisboa. Tel: 721254/721379/ 721475.
R	RUMANIA	ADMINISTRATIA ASIGURARILOR de STAT, Bucuresti, Str. Smirdan 5. Tel: 15.05.19.
E	SPAIN	OFICINA ESPANOLA de ASEGURADORES de AUTOMOVILES, Sagasta, 18 Madrid 4. Tel: 446. 0300.
S	SWEDEN	TRAFIKFORSAKRINGSFORENINGEN. Tegeluddsvagen 100, S-115 87 Stockholm. Tel: 06-783 7000.
CH	SWITZERLAND	SWISS GROUP OF MOTOR INSURERS, Mythenquai 2, 8002 Zurich. Tel: 01/205 21 21.
TN	TUNISIA	BUREAU AUTOMOBILE TUNISIEN, Square Avenue de Paris, Tunis. Tel: 256.800.
TR	TURKEY	TURKISH INSURANCE AND REINSURANCE ASSOCIATION MOTOR INSURANCE BUREAU, Osmanli Sokak No. 14/16, Taksim, Istanbul. Tel: 49.70.93.
YU	YUGOSLAVIA	UDRUZENJE OSIGURAVAJUCIH ORGANIZACIJA JUGO-SLAVIJE, 29 Novembra, 68-B Mezanin II. P.O. Box 428. 11000 Beograd. Tel: 011/750-359, 750-453, 751-389.

Appendix 2
Selective Glossary of Credit Finance Terms

Budget account agreement A debtor-creditor supplier agreement for running account credit with a credit threshold, with instalments including either a fixed charge for each transaction or a charge related to the price.

Conditional sale agreement An agreement for the sale of goods or land where the price is paid by instalments and ownership remains vested in the seller until certain conditions are met.

Consumer credit agreement One between an individual (the debtor) and any other person (the creditor) under which the creditor supplies credit to the debtor not exceeding £15,000.

Credit agreement A personal credit agreement which is secured on land or buildings or, indeed, a consumer credit agreement.

Debtor-creditor agreement A consumer credit agreement which is a regulated agreement but is not a debtor-supplier agreement.

Excepted agreement The following types of agreement are not included under Part V of the Consumer Credit Act 1974:
  (i)   bank overdraft
  (ii) agreement permitting temporary excess on a running account agreement
  (iii) unwritten debtor-creditor agreement to pay taxes and dues falling on death.

Excepted linked transaction A current or deposit account, guarantee of goods or a contract of insurance.

Hire-purchase agreement An agreement (not a conditional sale agreement) under which possession of goods is transferred in consideration for instalment payments and ownership passes on the occurrence of a specific event, eg the exercise of an option to purchase.

Modifying agreement One which is additional to, or seeks to vary, an existing agreement.

Multiple agreement One which, because it comes under

various categories of the Act, is to be treated as a number of separate agreements.

Non-commercial agreement One not made in the course of a business carried on by the creditor or hirer.

Personal credit agreement An agreement under which an individual is supplied with credit of any amount.

Regulated agreement A consumer credit agreement or consumer hire agreement which is not an exempt agreement nor a foreign agreement.

Unexecuted agreement A document which includes the terms of a suitable agreement awaiting due execution.

References

Bennion, Francis: *Consumer Credit Act Manual*, 3rd edn. Longman, 1986.

Brown, L: *A Manager's Guide to International Road Freighting*, 1st edn. Kogan Page, 1986.

Brown, R. E. G: *Employment Law in Road Transport*, Transport & Distribution Press Ltd, 1979.

Denning, Lord: *The Due Process of Law*, Butterworth, 1980.

Freight Magazine, Freight Transport Association.

Gartside, L: *Model Business Letters*, 3rd edn. MacDonald & Evans Ltd, 1981.

Goode, Roy: *Commercial Law*, Penguin, 1985.

Joseph, Michael: *The Conveyancing Fraud*, Michael Joseph, 1976.

Lowe, David: *A Study Manual of Professional Competence in Road Transport Management*, 4th edn. Kogan Page, 1984.

Lowe, David: *The Transport Manager's Handbook 1987*, Kogan Page, 1987.

O'Hare, John: *Civil Litigation*, 1st edn. Oyez Publishing Ltd, 1980.

Packer, Bill and Sandy, Colin: *Touche Ross Tax Guide for the Self Employed 1986/87*, Papermac edn., 1985.

Parkington, Martin: *Landlord and Tenant*, 2nd edn. Weidenfeld & Nicolson, 1980.

Price, Terry: *Practical Business Law*, Pan Books, 1982.

Pritchard, John: *The Penguin Guide to the Law*, 2nd edn. Penguin Books, 1985.

Rudinger, Edith: *Taking Your Own Case to Court or Tribunal*, Consumer Association, 1985.

The Sale of Goods Act 1979, annotated by Thomas, W. H., Sweet & Maxwell, 1980.

Saunders, John B (ed): *Mosely and Whitely's Law Dictionary*, 9th edn. Butterworth, 1977.

Sewell, Tim: lecture on *Consumer Credit – Entering the Agreement*, College of Law, 1985.

Theunissen, Andrew: *Guide to Successful Debt Collecting*, Rose Jordan Ltd, 1982.

Thomas, Bill: *Questions of Law*, Hamlyn Paperbacks, 1979.

Thomas, Colin: *Company Law*, Teach Yourself Books, 1982.

Walmsley, Keith (ed): *Company Law Handbook*, 4th edn. Butterworth, 1985.

Wedderburn, Lord: *The Worker and the Law*, 3rd edn. Penguin Books, 1986.

1987 Yearbook, Freight Transport Association Ltd, 1987.

Year-end Tax Planning for Companies, CCH Editions Ltd.

Index